Projectile Point Typology
Gila River Indian Community, Arizona

A draft of this volume of the Gila River Indian Community, Anthropological Research Papers was previously distributed by the Cultural Resource Management Program as P-MIP Technical Report No. 02-04.

Gila River Indian Community
Anthropological Research Papers
Number 2

Projectile Point Typology
Gila River Indian Community, Arizona

Chris Loendorf and Glen E. Rice

Gila River Indian Community
Cultural Resource Management Program
Sacaton, Arizona

About the Authors

CHRIS LOENDORF, (MA, Arizona State University) is a Project Director for the Gila River Indian Community Cultural Resource Management Program, and is also a Ph.D. student at Arizona State University.

GLEN E. RICE, (Ph.D. 1977, University of Washington) is on the faculty at Arizona State University and a consultant for the Cultural Resource Management Program of the Gila River Indian Community.

Cover: A sample of projectile points recovered during field investigations by the Cultural Resource Management Program, Gila River Indian Community, Arizona (shown slightly smaller than actual size).

ISBN: 0-9723347-1-8

TABLE OF CONTENTS

LIST OF FIGURES

LIST OF TABLES

FOREWORD

In 1994, staff of the Gila River Indian Community's Cultural Resource Management Program began the enormous task of archaeologically surveying 146,000 acres of the reservation. An archaeological inventory of this acreage was necessitated as part of the planning process prior to the construction of the Pima-Maricopa Irrigation Project. Unlike most of the modern landscape abutting metropolitan Phoenix, the 371,000 acres or approximately 600 square miles that comprise the reservation are largely undeveloped. Ground disturbance activities related to agriculture represent the primary development, which has impacted some 77,000 acres of the reservation. Fortunately, for the archaeologist working at Gila River, a majority of the lands were farmed only during historic times and have escaped the disturbances associated with modern agricultural land leveling methods. As a result, most of the large villages with associated public architecture, farmsteads, field houses, and specialized procurement locales located in the areas between villages remain relatively undisturbed. Because of this unique situation, archaeological survey has provided important insights about Archaic, Hohokam, and historic Akimel O'odham (Pima) and Pee Posh (Maricopa) land-use strategies, which are otherwise unavailable today in central Arizona.

This volume by Loendorf and Rice represents the first publication by the program of some of the vast numbers of artifacts collected by survey crews during the inventory of the 146,000 acres. They report on the nearly 1,000 projectile points or point preforms recovered from 195 of the over 1,000 recorded sites. The temporally sensitive stylistic types that comprise the collection demonstrate a long and complex use of the landscape. As the reader of this volume will learn, the middle Gila River valley was not an empty niche during Archaic period times as is amply demonstrated by projectile point styles. At the other end of the chronological sequence, the projectile point dataset provides an unparalleled opportunity to study the evolutionary development of post-classic, proto-historic, and historic projectile point styles. Nonetheless, we have only begun to scratch the surface when one considers the magnitude and significance of this important dataset. Subsequent studies of these projectile points with the addition of those acquired from excavation contexts will further refine the preliminary classification typologies presented. Detailed metric data and photographs of the points described in this volume have been included so that other researchers interested in prehistoric and historic lithic technology will have the opportunity to build upon the initial conclusions reached by Leondorf and Rice.

John C. Ravesloot, Coordinator
Cultural Resource Management Program

PREFACE

This document is the first of a multi-part series on the analysis of projectile points from the Gila River Indian Community (GRIC). Our design for the study of projectile points includes both classificatory (or categorical) and metric analyses. This volume focuses on the set of definitions and procedures used for the classificatory or categorical analysis. We intend to implement more than one metric analysis; the methods and results of such analyses are described in other volumes.

The classificatory analysis can be conducted in the abstract without reference to any particular database or population of projectile points. The diagnostic attributes for each class are described using words and text; illustrations are useful but they cannot be substituted for the textual definition. The purpose of the classificatory analysis is to provide a set of standard, well-defined, etic units that can be applied across regions. For instance, using the classification, a Pinto point in the Sonoran Desert will be identical to a Pinto point on the Colorado Plateau *with respect to the attributes defined as diagnostic for the Pinto style.* Aside from the attributes that are diagnostic for the class, the two Pinto points are of course likely to differ in a number of ways, and it is the objective of the metric analysis to examine that variability.

The metric analyses are the emic complement to the etic units of the classificatory analysis. The metric studies are performed with respect to particular populations of points (they cannot be performed in the abstract), and the results will therefore be different for each population. One purpose of the metric analyses is to explain the variability that exists between different classes within the same population, or between the same class in two different populations. Thomas (1981), for instance, used a quantitative analysis of metric attributes to establish absolute differences among projectile point types in the Monitor Valley; he developed a key that used metric attributes to group Monitor Valley points into types. In another example, Vaughn and Warren (1987) demonstrated that Pinto points in the Mojave Desert differed significantly in metric attributes from Pinto points in the Central Great Basin. Such quantitative comparisons are possible because the etic category of Pinto style can be applied to group projectile points in the different regions into the same type. Eventually, the results of metric analyses can be used to refine the distinctions made in the classificatory analysis, but this objective must await the accumulation of large, comparative data sets from different parts of the Southwest region.

Metric attributes will be used in the analysis of both style and performance characteristics; these analyses are discussed elsewhere. This volume focuses on establishing the categorical distinctions in point styles that are commonly used in the literature, and reviewing what is currently known about the age and distributions of those styles.

ACKNOWLEDGMENTS

The authors were helped by a number of people in preparing this report and we gratefully acknowledge their efforts on our behalf. Stacy Oliver and Bonny Rockette, laboratory directors in succession, developed repeated queries of the database, had the projectile points pulled from the collections for analysis and documentation, and oversaw the addition of our analyses to the database. Alana Ossa also helped with revisions and additions to the structure of the database. Tom Herrschaft assisted the laboratory directors in pulling the collections and did a great job as production editor in seeing this volume through to publication. Lorie Sinclair handled the time consuming task of scanning the projectile points for use on the CD-ROM, and her meticulous attention to detail is gratefully acknowledged. Thanks also to Randall Rhoades who conducted much of the first stage lithic analysis that was crucial for developing the database inventories. We have built on the previous research conducted by Mark Brodbeck and Charles Hoffman of the projectile points and bifaces in the Gila River Indian Community collections. Our thanks to Bob Neily for many useful conversations in which he shared his considerable knowledge about the archaeology of projectile point styles and the Greater Southwest.

The manuscript was reviewed by our peers Keith Kintigh, Patricia Crown, and Terry Majewski and we thank them for their thoughtful comments and for their help in improving the content of this document. Finally, our thanks to John Ravesloot, the Program Coordinator for the Gila River Indian Community Cultural Resource Management Program (GRIC-CRMP), who commented on and encouraged us through multiple drafts of this volume. It is because of his energy and vision as director of the Gila River Cultural Resources Management Program that we are able to participate in one of the most remarkable and challenging archaeological research and interpretive projects in the nation, and we thank him for that opportunity. To all of our colleagues, named and unnamed, for working with us on this volume and the project, you have our heartfelt thanks. Any errors or omissions remaining in this text after all of this help are our responsibility.

CHAPTER 1

ANALYSIS OF PROJECTILE POINTS: METHODS AND ISSUES

As of the summer of 2002, the Gila River Indian Community Cultural Resource Management Program (GRIC-CRMP) had recovered almost 1,000 projectile points or point preforms from the community during archaeological field investigations (Figure 1). This collection is comprised of artifacts recovered almost exclusively from the surface of sites, with few points from subsurface contexts. The classification system presented in this document is primarily intended to separate these points into temporally sensitive stylistic categories. Because determining the age of points recovered in surface collections is problematic, the chronological placement of the types in the classification system is largely based on previous research in the region.

Considerable consensus exists regarding the definition of Archaic period styles, because of their importance in chronological studies. However, there is not a similarly well-established classification system for points from the Ceramic period. Instead, researchers generally employ ad hoc types for any given collection. The lack of success in establishing point chronologies for the Ceramic period is at least partially due to the incomparability among classification schemes employed by different researchers.

In an attempt to break the pattern of idiosyncratic typologies, this document substantially incorporates the projectile point classification developed by Sliva (1997). However, some of these styles are not clearly differentiated from each other based on quantified point attributes (for example, Sedentary Intermediate Side-Notched and Late Classic Side-Notched), which necessitated the collapse of some categories. Appendix A lists the style assigned to each artifact and any comments. Appendix B provides scatterplots of the metric data for each point style with more than 5 examples. Scanned images of all projectile points are included as Appendix C. This was done to allow them to be classified differently, because there is so little consensus among Ceramic period categorical analyses. While helpful, scanned images of one point face are far from ideal, as it is generally difficult to identify breakage or other aspects that may dramatically affect interpretations of point style. For example, usewear and steep angle retouch are important factors for distinguishing drills from certain narrow projectile point styles; however, neither of these characteristics are readily apparent from the scanned images. To address this concern, metric and attribute data (including usewear and breakage variables) for each projectile point are presented in Appendix D. These data, however, are not discussed in detail in this volume.

This document represents the first step in the analysis of projectile points from the Gila River Indian Community; points are only assigned to a set of categorically defined

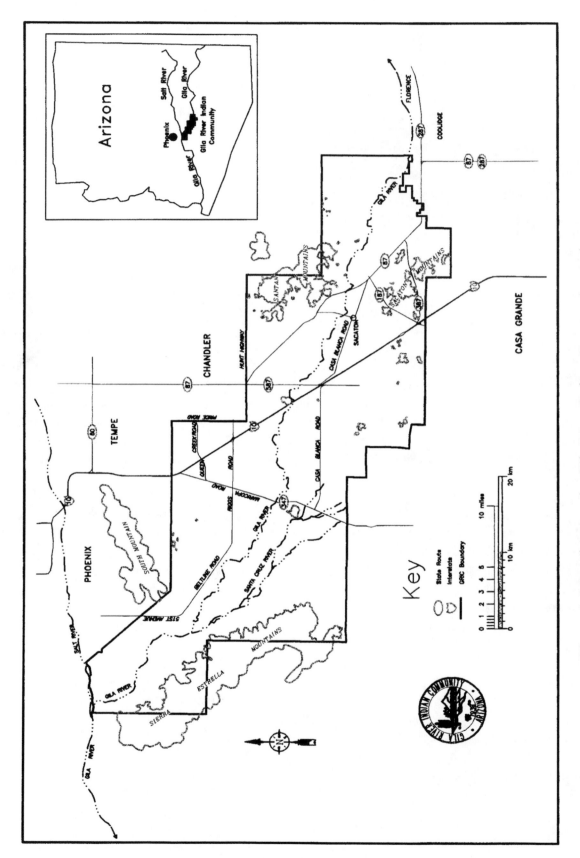

Figure 1. Map showing the Gila River Indian Community study area

styles at this stage. This process, in part, provides baseline data for analyses that will examine metric variation among these types. In addition, both diachronic and synchronic variation among morphological and metric attributes will be considered independently of these types. Before these analyses can proceed, however, point assemblages from excavated contexts in the study area are necessary. Both the categorical assignments and metric attributes of projectile points will be compared to independent absolute age estimates (for example, through the radiocarbon method) and stratigraphic associations as they become available.

LITHIC TECHNOLOGY

The prehistoric and historic inhabitants of the middle Gila River area appear to have practiced an expedient lithic technology in which relatively few retouched tools were manufactured. The retouched tool collection consists largely of projectile points in various stages of manufacture. In addition, small numbers of drills, perforators, scrapers of various types, spokeshaves, unifaces, and other bifaces are present.

Flaked-stone artifacts were analyzed in two stages. The first stage involved initial classification of the lithics according to material and lithic type. In the second stage, more detailed observations were recorded for the projectile points, including morphological characteristics and metric attributes. To control for inter-observer error, all Stage 2 analysis was completed by the lead author of this document.

A wide variety of projectile point styles are present in the Gila River flaked-stone collection. Projectile points in the collection appear to be styles that date to the Middle Archaic period (possibly as early as about 7000 B.P.) through the late Historic period (late nineteenth century A.D.). Both large Archaic-style projectile points and small Ceramic-period projectile points were identified in the collection. The larger Archaic points are thought to have been used on atlatl darts, whereas the smaller points were probably made for use on arrow shafts (Hoffman 1997; Shott 1996; Thomas 1978:470).

In this analysis, atlatl points were distinguished from arrow points on the basis of morphology and size. Archaic period styles are differently shaped from Ceramic period styles, except for a few simple shapes such as triangular points that are common occurrences in both periods. Shott (1996:298), in an analysis of hafted dart and arrow points recovered from dry cave deposits, found that the shoulder width was the most reliable discriminator between atlatl and arrow points. In our analysis, a histogram of shoulder width measurements of 622 completed points proved to be markedly bimodal, with the trough between modes falling at about 14 mm. Using this as the discriminating value, fully 96% of the large points had shoulder widths above this value and 96% of the small points had widths below this value. Thus about 4% (24 points out of 622) of the points may be incorrectly classified as to large versus small categories.

RAW MATERIALS

The size, shape, and fracture toughness of raw materials constrain both the reduction techniques that can be employed and the character of the resulting artifacts (Andrefsky 1994; Binford 1979; Parry and Kelly 1997). Consequently, it is necessary to consider raw material constraints in any lithic analysis. Fracture toughness is defined as the stress-intensity factor necessary to begin the propagation of a crack in the stone (Cotterell and Kamminga 1987:678), and this factor is a fundamentally crucial characteristic of flaked-stone raw materials.

Although oversimplified, a meaningful dichotomy may be drawn between fine- and coarse-grained materials. Fine-grained materials have a shiny or glasslike surface luster, whereas coarse-grained materials have a dull luster and visible grain. Coarse-grained materials usually have a much higher fracture toughness than do fine-grained materials (Andrefsky 1994). Consequently, prehistoric flint knappers appear generally to have employed fine-grained and coarse-grained materials for different tasks.

Because of their lower fracture toughness, fine-grained materials are well suited for thinning and shaping into patterned tool types. In contrast, the high fracture toughness of most coarse-grained materials makes them extremely difficult (if not impossible) to retouch by pressure flaking into patterned tool types. At the same time, high fracture toughness would have been advantageous for their use as expedient tools, because the working edges would have dulled much less quickly than more brittle, fine-grained materials. As a result, fine-grained materials are closely associated with the production of patterned tools, whereas coarse-grained materials appear generally to have been used for the production of expedient flake tools.

The Gila River Indian Community is located in the Basin and Range physiographic province of south-central Arizona. Northwest-southeast trending mountain ranges rise abruptly in this region from broad and flat basins filled with deep deposits of eroded sediments (Pierce 1985). These sedimentary basins are filled with thousands of feet of alluvial gravels, sands, and silts eroded from nearby mountain ranges. The mountains were formed by both the erosion of uplifted fault blocks and volcanic activity (Hendricks 1985). Although some ranges primarily consist of silicic to basaltic composition rocks (for example, basalt, andesite, rhyolite), most of the mountains are comprised of Precambrian granites, schists, and gneiss (Anderson 1992; Reynolds 1985; Wilson 1969).

Fine-grained lithic resources have relatively limited distributions throughout the Lower Sonoran Desert (Anderson 1992; Shackley 1988). The cryptocrystalline and fine-grained lithic materials present occur primarily in two forms: as primary, concentrated deposits of lithic materials, and as mixed, secondary geological deposits spread more diffusely across the landscape (Anderson 1992). Primary, concentrated deposits of fine-grained lithic materials are not common in the middle Gila River watershed. Larger deposits of low-fracture-toughness materials do occur in relatively nearby areas. Some of these resources include obsidian deposits associated with the Superior, Vulture, and Sauceda mountains volcanic fields in south-central Arizona (Peterson 1994; Shackley 1988), as well as chert deposits in several nearby regions.

Course-grained materials that are better suited for ground-stone artifacts and expedient lithic tools are much more abundant locally. For example, large primary deposits of vesicular basalt were available at Lone Butte, the Santan Mountains, Picture Rocks, the Vaiva Hills, the McDowell Mountains, the Gila Bend Mountains, and at several locations in the New River drainage (Anderson 1992; Hoffman and Doyel 1985; Wilson 1969; Wilson et al. 1969).

Local, secondary geological deposits, such as Pleistocene river gravels, bajada surfaces, and alluvial fans, provided the most widespread source of lithic raw materials. These deposits contain a variety of igneous, metamorphic, and sedimentary gravels. Fine-grained cherts and chalcedonies can occasionally occur in these deposits, but higher fracture-toughness materials such as quartzites, rhyolites, basalts, dacites, and other siliceous volcanics are more common (Anderson 1992). These lithic materials are generally small and randomly dispersed at a low density across extensive areas.

Pot-lid fracturing and heat-induced crazing on some projectile points in the collection suggest that heat treatment of raw materials occurred. This process is likely to have affected the appearance of some raw materials (Ahler 1983), but should not have substantially altered assignments to the generalized material types employed in this analysis. The classification system employed here did not systematically record the presence of heat treatment. Consequently, the incidence of this practice has not been quantified. From a technological standpoint, heat treatment alters the nature of some raw materials in at least two important ways. First and foremost, it reduces the fracture toughness of the material, making it easier to pressure flake (Ahler 1983; Whittaker 1994:72–74). Second, heat treatment induces fracturing along natural cleavage lines, which otherwise could cause accidental breakage during reduction.

Chert is the most common material used for projectile point manufacture: 38 percent of the recovered artifacts were identified as chert (Table 1). Although obsidian does not naturally occur in the project area (Bayman and Shackley 1999), obsidian is the next most common type, accounting for almost one-third (26%) of all projectile points. Basalt is the next most common material, with 19 percent of the collection; and 6 percent of the points are rhyolite. All other materials are uncommon, occurring in frequencies 5 percent or less.

In general, naturally occurring fine-grained materials appear to be rare in the study area; most locally available materials are coarser grained with higher fracture toughness. Consequently, most of the projectile points in the collection appear to be made from nonlocal raw materials. The presence of cores and flakes of materials that are clearly not local (for example, obsidian) suggests that in many instances nonlocal raw materials must have been transported into the study area. On the other hand, patterning in the raw material use for at least one point style also suggests the possibility that finished points were transported into the project area.

6

Table 1. Material Type by Point Size for Projectile Points and Preforms

Type	Indeterminate		Large		Small		TOTAL	
	N	%	N	%	N	%	N	%
Chert	13	54%	85	31%	271	39%	369	38%
Obsidian	4	17%	7	3%	248	36%	259	26%
Basalt	3	13%	98	36%	91	13%	192	20%
Rhyolite	2	8%	45	17%	9	1%	54	5%
Chalcedony	1	4%	3	2%	45	7%	48	5%
Quartzite	0	0%	13	5%	4	1%	17	2%
Quartz	1	4%	4	1%	12	2%	16	2%
Meta-basalt	0	0%	9	3%	2	0%	11	1%
Glass	0	0%	0	0%	8	1%	8	1%
Siltstone	0	0%	4	1%	0	0%	4	0%
Welded Tuff	0	0%	2	1%	0	0%	2	0%
Dacite	0	0%	1	0%	0	0%	1	0%
Tuff	0	0%	1	0%	0	0%	1	0%
TOTAL	24		272		687		983	

Note: Percentages are for column totals.

Raw material choices differ dramatically between the large Archaic-style projectile points and small Ceramic-period projectile points. In general, finer-grained materials appear to have been preferred for the manufacture of small points. For example, less than 3 percent of the large points are made from obsidian, whereas this material is one of the most commonly identified for small points (36% of the collection). Variation in material type by point size is probably the result of several factors. First, larger points can be made with both soft and hard hammer reduction techniques, whereas it is difficult to produce small points without the use of pressure flaking. Because it is difficult or impossible to pressure flake coarse-grained materials, they may have only rarely been used for small-point manufacture. Second, the high fracture toughness of coarse-grained materials would have helped decrease point breakage for large points. This may have been less of a concern for small points, because of their reduced size and the higher velocities of arrows compared with the atlatl darts that probably carried the larger points. Third, coarse-grained materials are more commonly available locally, and the additional effort required to acquire nonlocal fine-grained materials may have limited their use to smaller point styles.

Raw material types also vary between different styles of projectile points (Table 2). In general, styles that were made at a given time generally were produced from similar types of raw materials, causing variation in raw material use that is apparent between time periods (Table 3). This temporal patterning is generally consistent with observations made elsewhere and supports the chronological validity of the classification system, at least at a gross level.

Table 2. Material Type by Point Style

Type	Basalt	Chalcedony	Chert	Dacite	Glass	Meta-basalt	Obsidian	Quartz	Quartzite	Rhyolite	Siltstone	Tuff	Welded Tuff	TOTAL
Indeterminate	3	1	13				4	1		2				24
Indeterminate Large Point	28	2	35			7	3	2	6	15	1	1	2	102
Mojave Lake	1													1
Silver Lake	2									2				4
Chiricahua	7		7						1	5	1			21
San Jose-Pinto A	19		7				1		1					28
San Jose-Pinto B	6								1					7
Gypsum	3		3	1				1		1				9
Cortaro	1	1	10							2				14
Shouldered Teardrop	6		1				1			1				9
Stemmed Teardrop	9					1			1	1				12
San Pedro	4		8			1		1	3	9	1			27
Cienega Flared										1				1
Cienega Long	7		2							5	1			15
Cienega Short	2		8				1			1				12
Cienega Stemmed	3		2				1			1				7
Indeterminate Small Point	25	18	98		1	2	83	8	2	3				240
Stemmed Barbed			2											2
Stemmed Shouldered			2							1				3
Stemmed Tanged		1	6											7
Wide Side-Notch			9				4	1						14
Intermediate Side-Notch	1	4	14				55			3				77
Narrow Side-Notch			10											10
Upper Side-Notch			2				1							3
Middle Side-Notch			14				4							18
Flanged	3	1	7				9		1					21
Bulbous Base			1				2							3
Concave Blade		4	17				15	2						38
Straight Blade Serrated	1						7	1						9
Concave Base Triangular	3	4	2				2							11
Long Triangular	6	1	6											13
Thin Triangular	1		7				1							9
Sraight Base Triangular	23	3	14		2		19		1	2				64
U-shaped Base Triangular	24	8	56		5		46			1				140
Eccentric	1	1	6											8
TOTAL	**189**	**49**	**369**	**1**	**8**	**11**	**259**	**17**	**17**	**56**	**4**	**1**	**2**	**983**

Table 3. Material Type by Estimated Period of Manufacture

Period	Basalt	Chalcedony	Chert	Obsidian	Rhyolite
Early Archaic	60%	0%	0%	0%	40%
Middle Archaic	56%	1%	30%	2%	11%
Late Archaic	30%	0%	35%	3%	32%
Pre-Classic	0%	10%	47%	39%	4%
Classic	11%	5%	35%	49%	0%
Protohistoric/ Historic	24%	6%	36%	33%	1%

Several trends are apparent in these data. First, basalt is the most common material for both Early and Middle Archaic projectile points. The use of basalt then declined until after the Classic period, when it accounts for nearly one quarter of the collection. Chert was popular throughout the sequence. Chert use peaked during the pre-Classic period, comprising nearly half of all the points from this time. Rhyolite was not commonly employed, but its use peaked during the Late Archaic period, largely because San Pedro points tend to be made from this material. The high incidence of rhyolite for only a single point style suggests that San Pedro points may have been brought to the study area as finished products.

Obsidian use appears to have peaked during the Classic period in the study area. Other researchers have also suggested that obsidian use peaked during the Classic period (Bayman and Shackley 1999; Peterson 1994:103; Rice et al. 1998:110).

Chalcedony was not commonly employed throughout the sequence. Its use peaked at less than 10 percent of the collection during the pre-Classic period, when chert use predominated, which is unsurprising given that these two materials often co-occur at source areas.

In general, widely diverse materials were employed after the Classic period, when long-standing trade networks may have been disrupted by dramatic demographic changes. The diversity of materials is consistent with the suggestion that at this time flint knappers were forced to scavenge fine-grained materials from previous components of sites (confer, Russell 1908:111).

GEOMORPHOLOGICAL EFFECTS ON PROJECTILE POINT DISTRIBUTION

Because the collection was almost exclusively recovered from surface contexts, which include landforms of differing ages, consideration of geomorphological processes that may alter the spatial distribution of projectile points is especially important. The effects of erosion and deposition have a considerable influence on the spatial patterns of projectile points dating to different periods. Old landforms may yield recent points, but younger landforms are unlikely to exhibit older point styles on the modern ground surface. Consequently, the apparent frequency and distribution of point styles through time are affected. Put another way, the sampled area varies with age, such that older point styles can be recovered only from a subset of the surfaces on which younger points would be expected to occur.

The situation is further complicated by the fact that the settlement pattern of a group, among a number of different variables, affects both the number and location of sites chosen for occupation on a yearly basis. For example, bottomlands that experience regular flooding and erosion are unlikely to be selected as sites on which to build structures for permanent year-round occupation (Waters and Ravesloot 2001:291). In addition, these lands may be important locations for agricultural fields, and occupation would remove land from production. On the other hand, more mobile groups might prefer the same bottomlands for seasonal occupations, especially during the driest portions of the year. Because permanent occupations are more likely to be placed in locations that do not experience regular flooding and erosion, they are more likely to be preserved in the archaeological record. In contrast, at least some of the occupations of mobile groups are likely to be in locations where remains are either destroyed or buried under substantial deposition. Consequently, surface evidence for hunter and gatherer occupations along rivers would be less likely to be preserved than those of sedentary agriculturists, who lived in more permanent structures.

Fortunately, a multiyear project mapped and dated the Holocene and Pleistocene landforms across the extent of the Gila River Indian Community (Waters and Ravesloot 2000). The main landform categories include a set of alluvial terraces along the Gila River and its tributaries, an extensive area of Holocene eolian sand sheet and dune fields, and piedmonts (bajadas) that are either Holocene or Pleistocene in age.

Ages for the terraces along the Gila River were estimated using the radiocarbon method, but other landforms that have not been dated are assigned only to general geological periods, such as early Holocene or Pleistocene, based on their relative degree of soil development and other factors (Waters 1986). The eolian sand sheet and dune fields may have been deposited during the early Holocene, possibly ending around roughly 5000 B.C.

The Pleistocene fans are more than 40,000 years old and predate human occupation of the New World. The approximate ages of the surfaces of the main landform categories are as follows:

Landform	Designation	Age of Surface
Gila River Channel	(T-0)	A.D. 1650 +
Lower Gila River Terrace	(T-1)	A.D. 1100–1650
Upper Gila River Terrace	(T-2)	A.D. 1100
Holocene Eolian Sand Sheet	(Hess)	Early Holocene
Holocene Eolian Dune Fields	(Hed)	Early Holocene
Holocene Fans	(Hf)	Early Holocene
Pleistocene Fans	(Pf)	Pleistocene

The greatest temporal range of projectile points will occur on the surface of the oldest geomorphic landforms. The younger landforms will generally have only more recent archaeological remains. The current, active surface of the Gila River channel (T-0) will not contain projectile points except possibly as secondary deposits derived from erosion of the upper terraces.

The T-1 terrace was created in most places by the erosion of a unit that was deposited during the last 1,000 years, and in such locations the surface of T-1 is likely to have projectile points from the Sedentary through Historic periods. (In a few places the T-1 terrace is formed by the erosion of an older landform, and Pioneer-period or even Middle to Late Archaic projectile points may be found there.)

The T-2 terrace has been developing for the last 18,000 years, and although a period of stabilization took place around A.D. 1100, some deposition has occurred within the last 500 years. Classic, Protohistoric, and Historic sites and projectile points are likely to occur on the surface of the T-2 terrace; by contrast, pre-Classic, Late Archaic, and Middle Archaic sites and artifacts are buried in the T-2 terrace. Some Middle Archaic points have been found on this surface, which may have resulted from cultural transport of points or exposure by erosion or historic excavation (Ravesloot and Waters 2004).

Sites and artifacts dating to the Middle Archaic through the Protohistoric period are known to occur on the Holocene sand sheet and dune fields (Ravesloot and Waters 2004:209), but Paleo-Indian or Early Archaic points have not been found in these locations. This suggests that perhaps portions of the sand sheet and dune fields had stabilized by the Middle Archaic period, although other areas continue to be currently active. Finally, materials from the Clovis to the Modern period may be found on the Pleistocene fans, which date prior to 40,000 years ago.

PROJECTILE POINT CLASSIFICATION

Archaeologists have suggested many explanations for variation in the appearance of projectile points. A partial listing of these sources of variation includes, style in any of its various suggested manifestations; usewear or reworking after breakage; individual differences in motor skills resulting in deviation from an ideal form; low standards of conformity to ideals; random drift from norms as a function of time or space; raw material constraints; improvement or change in ballistic performance requirements (Shott 1996); variation in prey size (Churchill 1993); change in design criteria related to mechanical stress resistance (Shott 1996:281); point variants made for ritual and mundane purposes; toy point variants (Bonnichsen and Keyser 1982); and measurement or classification error by researchers.

Another possibility not generally emphasized by archaeologists is that at a given point in time people may have made different types of points for different purposes. Specifically, it is possible that different types of stone projectile points were made for hunting and warfare (Ahler 1992). This possibility will be examined in greater detail as a part of continuing

GRIC-CRMP investigations. A further additional factor in point morphology variation is that notching style may have partially been a pragmatic response to modifying the stem so that it could be hafted (Flenniken and Raymond 1985:606).

These potential factors are not mutually exclusive. On the contrary, more than one of them almost certainly influenced variation among points. Consequently, no single explanation should be taken as the monolithic cause of variation in projectile point collections. Regardless of these reasons for variation, projectile point morphology clearly changed through time, and typologies can be used to classify this variation in a way that provides meaningful chronological data.

Table 4 lists attributes that were recorded for each point. Figure 2 is a depiction of the terms used to refer to aspects of the points. Metric attributes are also indicated on the figure for reference purposes. These measurements are discussed only as summary statistics in this volume but are among the metric attributes that will be used in future quantitative analyses. The intent of the projectile point classification system presented in this document is to employ morphological variation among projectile points to define stylistic types and to begin considering the temporal duration and spatial distribution of each of the styles. Temporal control of stylistic variation is still poorly understood in the project area, and one of the primary objectives of subsequent research will be to further refine our understanding of both the styles and their associated age ranges.

The analysis first segregated the projectile point collection using Whittaker's (1984) distinction between small and large point complexes. Of the 708 completed projectile points recovered during the project, 572 were assigned to classes in the typology. Appendix A lists the production stage for each artifact in the collection. Because of their unfinished character, preforms were not generally assigned to classes in the typology and are listed as "indeterminate" in the appendix. In many cases, however, it was possible to suggest whether the preform was intended to be a large or small point. In total, 239 artifacts were classified as indeterminate small projectile points and 101 artifacts were considered indeterminate large projectile points because they were either too fragmentary or not completed.

For a projectile point style to be useful chronologically, the following three criteria must be met: the points included in the type should consistently share a set of physical (observable) attributes; the set of shared attributes should have a continuous distribution in time (Vaughn and Warren 1987:199) as demonstrated through stratigraphic and chronological studies; and the physical characteristics used to define types should be mutually exclusive such that all styles can be differentiated.

The first and third criteria are satisfied by definitions provided in Tables 5 and 20. At this time we have not determined if the types in the classification scheme meet the second criteria because the necessary distributional data have yet to be collected. Tables 5 and 20 essentially provide a hypothesized set of distinctions that will be verified and possibly modified as data (stratigraphic relationships, seriational patterns, absolute dates, spatial distributions) are collected. The following discussion of the point styles focuses on what is

Table 4. Attributes Used in the Classification of Archaic Point Styles

Diagnostic Criteria and Associated Attributes

Point Shape
>   Teardrop: convex blade margins that taper asymmetrically from the base to the tip.
>   Lanceolate: lower blade margins are parallel and taper in a curve to the tip.
>   Triangular: straight blade margins with the maximum width at the base.
>   Diamond: trapezoidal shape with shoulders (maximum blade width) near the midpoint of the blade.

Haft Treatment
>   Notch: depressions in the blade margin that are at least as deep as wide (Holmer 1986).
>   Side-notched: notches are approximately perpendicular to the long axis of the point, and the base width is equal to or greater than the shoulder width.
>   Corner-notched: notches are at an angle of less than 90 degrees to the long axis of the point and the base width is less than the shoulder width.
>   Corner/Side-notched: notches are perpendicular to the long axis of the point, and the base width is less than the shoulder width.
>   Stemmed: the hafted portion is separated from the blade by a shoulder.
>   Unnotched:lacks notching or a stem; the haft element is not differentiated from the blade by either a shoulder or notch.

Stem Shape
>   Expanding: base width is greater than the minimum haft element width.
>   Straight: base width is approximately equal to the minimum haft element width.
>   Contracting: base width is the minimum haft element width.

Base Shape
>   Concave: the basal corners are lower than the center of the base.
>   Convex: the basal corners are higher than the center of the base.
>   Straight: the basal corners and central portion of the base form an approximately straight line (as straight as possible given irregularities of flake scars).
>   Pointed: the basal corners meet.

Shoulder Shape
>   Obtuse Angle: the junction of the blade and haft element is greater than a right angle.
>   Abrupt: the junction of the blade and haft element forms a right angle.
>   Barbed: the junction of the blade and haft element form an acute angle.

Proportionate Criteria
>   Haft Element Width: See Figure 2 for location of measurement
>   Shoulder Width: See Figure 2 for location of measurement
>   Base Width: See Figure 2 for location of measurement

Serrated Edge
>   Present: Blade has adjacent small notches forming teeth along the edge.
>   Absent: Edge of blade is not serrated.

Blade Margin Shape
>   Straight: The blade margins define a straight line between the basal corners and the tip.
>   Concave: The blade margins define concave lines between the basal corners and the tip.
>   Convex: The margins of the blade define convex lines between basal corners and the tip.

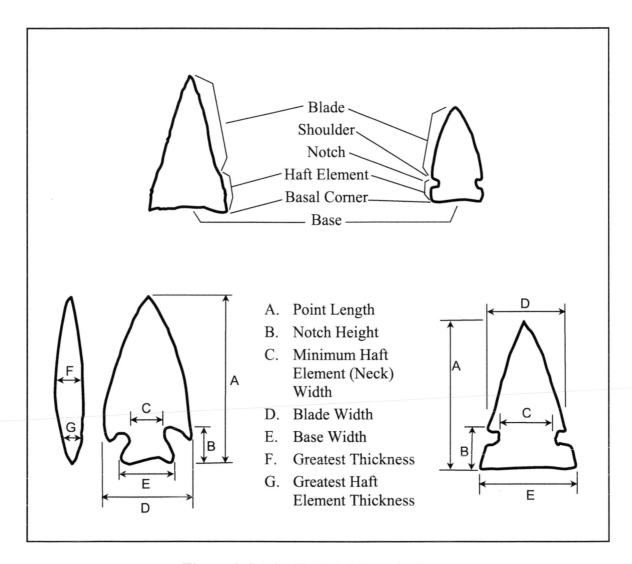

Figure 2. Projectile Point Terminology.

currently known about the temporal utility of these types (Figure 3), which will be modified as GRIC-CRMP investigations provide additional data for the middle Gila region.

To facilitate comparisons with projectile points collected during other projects, points were classified following the system devised by Sliva (1997) for central and southern Arizona. In addition, scanned images of all points are presented in Appendix C. When possible, comparisons are made with the typologies employed by Hoffman (1997) and Justice (2002) in their large regional analyses of points, both of which included collections from Snaketown. The lack of consistency in classification schemes for Hohokam projectile points complicates any comparisons with collections from elsewhere in the region. In contrast, the more consistent application of types for Archaic points facilitates more detailed comparisons with previous research.

When considering the projectile point sample from the middle Gila, it is important to emphasize again that the collection was derived almost exclusively (97%) from surface

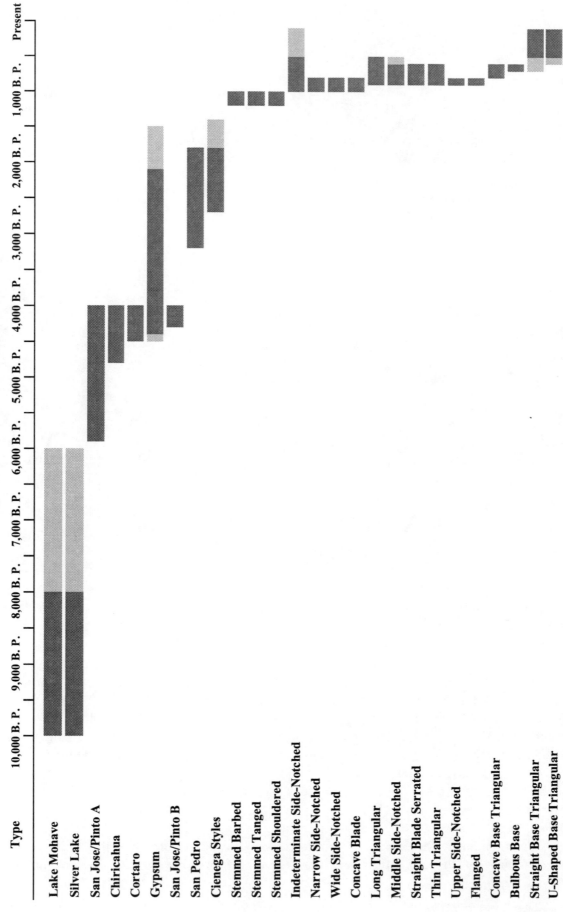

Figure 3. Age Estimates for Point Styles in the Collection, Gila River Indian Community

Light shading refers to poorly documented intervals of time.

contexts. This has probably biased the sample in several important ways. First, because they are generally covered by deposition, artifacts in contexts such as house floors or burial features are less likely to be exposed on the modern ground surface. Consequently, the sample may be skewed toward artifacts from middens or other contexts that are less likely to be buried. Second, recent artifacts are more likely to be exposed on the modern ground surface, because they have experienced a shorter period in which they may have been buried by deposition, redeposited by erosion, or collected by people using the area at a later date. Third, during the survey no artifacts were collected from areas with human bone; consequently, any artifacts potentially associated with human remains were not sampled.

Production Sequence

To make a projectile point, it is necessary to go through a series of steps. Despite the variety of reduction strategies that can be employed, the process can be classified into a series of stages. Whittaker (1994:153–159) has defined four stages in this process, which were simplified to three categories (early, nearly completed, and completed) for the current analysis. In addition, Whittaker defines Stage 0 as selecting a suitable blank for the desired point. This blank must be larger than the intended size of the point and should be relatively flat. This step is referred to as "Stage 0 because it is not possible to recognize an unworked blank in archaeological sites" (Whittaker 1994:153).

Several characteristics were employed to distinguish point preforms from completed points, including the presence of step fractures or other factors that would preclude further thinning, symmetry, and the presence or absence of usewear. In this analysis, preforms were subjectively classified as either early stage or nearly completed (late stage). Early stage preforms were defined as relatively flat artifacts with invasive retouch on one or more margins. These artifacts lack macroscopically visible usewear and are more irregular than late stage preforms, or nearly completed points. It is often difficult to distinguish early stage preforms from a variety of different artifact types including unifaces and bifacial knives. This is especially true for the large point collection, where preforms may easily be misclassified. However, roughly equal proportions of the three point stages were identified for large and small points (see below), suggesting that this possibility was not a factor in the current analysis.

Nearly completed points were defined as relatively small artifacts with invasive bifacial retouch on more than two margins. These artifacts also lack usewear. Because notches are generally added in the final manufacturing stages (Whittaker 1994:159), it is frequently difficult to separate completed points that lack notches from late stage preforms that were discarded prior to notching. Step fractures were in part used to differentiate discarded late stage preforms from completed points. Irregular edges and an overall lack of symmetry were also used to separate late stage preforms from completed points.

Projectile point preforms constitute approximately 25 percent of the point collection. Roughly equal proportions of large and small point preforms were identified (Table 5). The consistency in the proportions of the stages for large and small projectile types suggests that late stage preforms were not frequently misclassified as completed points. This suggestion is supported by the observation that unnotched points, which are easily misclassified as late stage preforms, are common in the small point collection but rare in the large point collection.

Table 5. Point Size by Stage of Production

Stage	Indeterminate		Large		Small		TOTAL
Indeterminate	5	17%	4	1%	6	1%	11
Finished	8	29%	216	77%	484	72%	708
Nearly Finished	7	25%	30	11%	99	15%	136
Early Stage	8	29%	31	11%	85	12%	124
TOTAL	28		281		674		983

Note: All percentages are for column totals.

Serration

Serration of point edges was sometimes practiced; 215 points with serrated edges were collected, and 30 percent of all completed projectile points had this form of edge treatment. Serration was identified on both large and small projectile points of various styles. Most other technological factors vary by point size, but nearly equal proportions of large points (30%) and small points (31%) were serrated. The edges of unnotched, side-notched, corner-notched, and stemmed points were all sometimes serrated. This variability suggests that serration may have been done for more than one reason, but the reasons for this practice remain unclear.

One possibility suggested by the early Jesuit missionary Fr. Ignaz Pfefferkorn is that edges of projectile points used in warfare were serrated "to effect a more painful and dangerous wound" (Pfefferkorn 1989:202). In any case, the apparent lack of patterning in serration with respect to point size or haft element treatment suggests that this attribute is a poor indicator of temporal variation in point morphology.

CHAPTER 2

LARGE PROJECTILE POINT COMPLEX

A total of 167 projectile points was assigned to types that are thought to date primarily to the Archaic or Early Formative periods (Table 6). An additional 102 fragmentary or unfinished large points are probably also from this same span of time. Although no examples of Paleo-Indian and only 5 possible Early Archaic points have been identified, the rarity of these styles is probably the result, in part, of geomorphological factors (Waters and Ravesloot 2000; Ravesloot and Waters 2002). The sample of Middle Archaic points is comparatively large, with 100 examples in the collection. A total of 62 points is thought to be primarily Late Archaic or Early Agricultural styles.

Table 6. Definitions of Large (Archaic) Point Styles Used in This Volume

Silver Lake (Armagosa): Triangular shaped, straight or contracting stem, convex base, obtuse shoulders, maximum haft element width less than maximum shoulder width.

Lake Mojave (Jay/Contracting Stem): Diamond shaped, contracting stem, pointed or convex base, maximum haft element width equal to maximum shoulder width.

Chiricahua: Triangular shaped blade, side-notched, concave to straight base, abrupt or rounded shoulder, base width greater than maximum shoulder width.

Pinto–San Jose A: Triangular shaped blade, straight or expanding stem, concave base, rounded to abrupt shoulders, haft element width less than maximum shoulder width.

Pinto–San Jose B: Triangular shaped, expanding stem, concave base, barbed shoulders and barbed basal corners, minimum haft element width less than maximum shoulder width, (frequently basal width is about equal to the maximum shoulder width).

Gypsum: Triangular shaped blade, tapering stemmed, pointed to convex base, abrupt shoulders, maximum stem (haft element) width less than maximum blade width.

Cortaro: Triangular shaped, not notched or stemmed, concave or straight based, rounded or abrupt basal corners, base width is the maximum point width.

Shouldered Teardrop: Teardrop shaped, abrupt shoulder, straight to contracting stem, base width is less than maximum width of point.

Stemmed Teardrop: Teardrop shape, obtuse shoulders, short stem, convex or straight base, minimum width of haft element is less than maximum shoulder width (similar to Silver Lake, the difference is that point must be leaf-shaped with convex blade margins).

San Pedro: Lanceolate or triangular shaped blade, corner/side-notched, abrupt shoulders, straight to convex base, maximum width of haft element is less than maximum shoulder width. Compared to Cienega Long, the notches are shallower and broader, without the diagonal angle to the long axis of the point (Huckell 1995:54).

Continued

Table 6. Definitions of Large (Archaic) Point Styles Used in This Volume *(Continued)*

Cienega Long: Triangular shaped blade, corner-notched, abrupt or barbed shoulders, convex base, neck width less than maximum shoulder width (Huckell 1995:51–53). Point length is greater than 30 mm. The width of the hafting device is considerably smaller than that of the San Pedro; in one study Huckell (1995:52) found the minimum width of the hafting element on Cienega points (e.g. 7.4 +/-1.3 mm) was considerably smaller than that of the San Pedro points (e.g. 16.0 +/-2.6 mm).

Cienega Flared: Triangular shaped with concave blade margins, corner notched, barbed shoulders, convex base, maximum width of hafting element is less than maximum shoulder width and point length is greater than 30 mm.

Cienega Short: Triangular shaped, corner notched, barbed or abrupt shoulders, convex base, maximum width of hafting element is less than shoulder width, and point length is less than 30 mm.

Cienega Stemmed: Triangular shaped, straight sided stem, convex base, abrupt or barbed shoulders, maximum width of hafting element is less than maximum shoulder width.

Haft treatment varies substantially between the large and small point collections (Table 7). Stemmed and corner-notched points are substantially more common in the large point collection, whereas side-notched and unnotched points are dramatically more common in the small point collection. Differences in stem treatment are probably the result of several factors including stylistic variation, performance issues, mechanical stress, and technological factors.

Table 7. Stem Treatment Frequency by Point Size

Stem Treatment	Large Point	Small Point
Corner-Notched	33%	1%
Stemmed	47%	4%
Side-Notched	12%	31%
Unnotched	8%	64%

The source of these Archaic projectile points is frequently problematic. Many of the Archaic points were recovered from sites with extensive evidence for occupation after the Archaic period. At least two possible explanations exist for the presence of older points on sites that were used more recently. First, the later inhabitants may have collected the points from elsewhere and reused them or kept them as curiosities. Second, these points may be associated with earlier occupation of the site area that is difficult to identify, in part, because Archaic collections lack diagnostic ceramics that are crucial temporal markers.

Early Archaic Styles

Although only five projectile points in the GRIC collection were attributed to styles thought to be from the Early Archaic, a discussion of Early Archaic styles is included here in anticipation of the eventual discovery of Early Archaic components in the Gila River Indian Community.

Lake Mojave and Silver Lake Styles

The earliest Archaic point styles in the Mojave, Sonoran and Chihuahuan deserts are stemmed with convex bases (Mabry et al. 1998:55; Haury 1950:203) and are subdivided into the *Lake Mojave* and the *Silver Lake* styles (Amsden 1935; Huckell 1984:112; Haury 1950:202–203; Mabry 1998:55). These co-occur in assemblages in the Mojave Basin (Mabry 1998:55) and the distinction between them is slight, having to do with the degree to which the stem is inset from the shoulder.

The Lake Mojave style (Figure 4a and 4b) is a diamond shaped point with a shoulder high up the blade; the stem tapers smoothly from the shoulder towards either a pointed base or a rounded base with rounded basal corners (Amsden 1935; Mabry 1998:55; Huckell 1984:112). There are short and long-stemmed varieties. The blade portion of the points can be considerably shorter than the stem, apparently because the points were frequently re-sharpened while hafted (Huckell 1984:116–118). One poor example of a Lake Mojave point with a rounded base (Figure 4b) and none with a pointed base (Figure 4a) have been recovered from the study area.

The Silver Lake style (Figure 4c) also has a stem with a convex base but the top of the stem is inset from the shoulder, creating a more pronounced shoulder than the Lake Mojave style. The stems are straight sided to sloping, and the basal corners can be abrupt (Jenkins 1987:217) or rounded (Haury 1950:202). Four examples of this style have been found in very different areas of the Community; three of them were associated with Ceramic period sites and one was an isolated find.

The Ventana-Armagosa I style from the Red Sand stratum in Ventana Cave (Haury 1950:202-203) is indistinguishable on these criteria from the Silver Lake style. The Jay style in New Mexico (Irwin-Williams 1973) resembles the Lake Mojave style with a rounded base, although with its slightly more pronounced shoulders it can also resemble the Silver Lake Style. The dating of the Jay style as given by Irwin-Williams (1967) is considerably later (6500 to 5500 B.C.) than for other areas, but possibly these dates are not tree-ring calibrated. Calibration would bring them closer to 8500 to 7500 years B.P. (Mabry et al. 1998:59). Matson (1991:144-145) recommends not incorporating these dates and the description of the Jay phase into models for the Southwest until the primary data from the Cuervo Arroyo project are published and are available for evaluation. Recent researchers in the Sonoran Desert have tended to refer to these as *Tapering Stemmed* styles to avoid the confusion of the multiple names (Bayham et al. 1986; Huckell 1984:112, 116; Lorentzen 1998:142).

At Ventana Cave, the Silver Lake style (called Ventana-Armagosa I) occurs in the Red Sand deposit that is not dated directly, but is bracketed between 8700 B.P. (radiocarbon ages from the stratum beneath the Red Sand) and 6000 B.P. (Huckell 1996b:331). The Midden stratum above the Red Sand stratum (and separated from it by a sterile stratum of

Figure 4. Early and Middle Archaic Point Styles from the Gila River Indian Community: a) Schematic Lake Mojave pointed base; b) Schematic Lake Mojave rounded base; c) Silver Lake; d) Chiricahua side-notched large projectile point; e) San Jose–Pinto type A variant; f) San Jose–Pinto type B variant; g) Gypsum; h) Cortero.

talus) contains Pinto points that are dated in the Sonoran Desert to about 6000 B.P. Thus, this is a possible start date for the Midden stratum, and consequently the termination date of the lower Red Sand stratum would need to be earlier. The Red Sand stratum at Ventana Cave is a rare case in Arizona where the early stemmed styles are shown to be stratigraphically earlier than the Pinto stemmed styles; in the northern part of the state, Lake Mojave and Silver Lake styles co-occur in deposits with Pinto points and may not have been antecedents to the Pinto style.

The Lake Mojave and Silver Lake styles appeared in the Mojave Desert as early as 10,000 B.P. (Douglas et al. 1988; Mabry et al. 1998:55) and were still in use around 8400 B.P. when Pinto styles first appeared. By 8000 B.P., Lake Mojave and Silver Lake styles were no longer in use in the Mojave Desert (Jenkins 1987:228–229). The Mojave Desert data provide insights into the dating of the Silver Lake style at Ventana Cave, suggesting that the date of the Red Sand stratum is likely to fall towards the early end of the bracket, possible between 8700 B.P. and 8000 B.P. Since Lake Mojave and Silver Lake styles also occur in the basal portions of the Midden stratum, this suggests that the start date for the stratum might be earlier than 8000 B.P.

Lake Mojave and Silver Lake styles were found as surface artifacts in the Picacho area in the Sonoran Desert (Bayham et al. 1986) and were excavated from shallow sites in the Santa Rosita Mountains of the Chihuahuan Desert (Huckell 1984), but neither case contributed to the independent dating of the points. Moreover, in these contexts they co-occurred with the Pinto Basin and other styles of Archaic points, and as a consequence they could not be established as antecedent styles. Without the evidence from Ventana Cave, the sequence of Early Archaic styles in the Sonoran Desert would not differ from that currently recorded on the Colorado Plateau.

Mike Waters (1986b) has contributed considerably to an understanding of the Early Archaic through his reanalysis of the Archaic period deposits in Whitewater Draw in southeastern Arizona. Using the results of 12 radiocarbon dates, Waters dated Sulphur Spring deposits between 8140 and 9900 B.P. Although only four fragmented projectile points were actually recovered from Sulphur Spring components, the two basal fragments could be examples of the tapering stem style (Mabry 1998:58–59).

These two styles are hallmarks of the Lake Mojave complex in the Mojave Desert and the San Dieguito complex in the Lower Colorado River valley and San Diego area of southern California (Warren 1967; Mabry 1998:56–57). The San Dieguito complex with Lake Mojave and Silver Lake styles has been dated at the Harris site near San Diego between 9000 and 8500 B.P. (Warren 1967) and in the San Joaquin valley at 8200 to 7600 B.P. (Fredrickson and Grossman 1977; cited in Mabry et al. 1998:57). Haury (1950:201–204) attributed the presence of these styles of stemmed points in Ventana Cave to contact with California.

Sources on the dating of the Lake Mojave and Silver Lake styles in the Mojave Desert and at Whitewater Draw in the Chihuahuan Desert are as follows (Mabry 1998:53–64):

SITE NAME (Reference)	DATE RANGE
Mojave Desert:	
Shore line of Lake Mojave (Warren and Ore 1978)	10,270 B.P.
Fort Irwin (Douglas et al. 1988)	9500 to 8500 B.P.
Rogers Ridge Site (Jenkins 1987)	10,000 to 8000 B.P.
Chihuahuan Desert:	
Whitewater Draw (Waters 1986b)	9300 to 8100 B.P.

Important research efforts include finding additional stratified or single component sites that establish the Lake Mojave and Sliver Lake styles as antecedent to the Pinto styles in the southern deserts, or alternatively build a larger sample of cases showing that the Pinto styles and the tapering stemmed styles appeared contemporaneously (as they apparently do on the Colorado Plateau and in the Central Mountains). It is also important to obtain absolute ages of these styles within each area.

Table 8. Average Dimensions for Lake Mojave and Silver Lake Points in the Collection

Attribute	Range	Average	Sample Size
Length	32.3mm- 43.8 mm	38.9 mm	n=4
Neck Width	10.0 mm– 16.3 mm	13.4 mm	n=5
Greatest Thickness	4.9 mm– 6.3 mm	5.7 mm	n=5
Base Width	9.2 mm– 16.3 mm	11.9 mm	n=5
Blade Width	16.5 mm– 22.7 mm	19.7 mm	n=5

Middle Archaic Styles

The typology includes five different Middle Archaic types, two of which were split into two variants each, making a total of seven Middle Archaic styles. Probable Middle Archaic points from the study area exhibit a number of similarities with collections from elsewhere in the region; however, the frequency of styles may vary somewhat. In particular, teardrop-shaped points may be unusually common in the study area.

Chiricahua

A total of 21 Chiricahua points were identified in the collection. These large projectile points have side notches near the base (Figure 4d). Point bases are generally concave, with most examples exhibiting deeply concave bases. A few examples (15%) with straight bases were also recorded. Shoulder treatment is generally abrupt, and rounded or sloping examples are uncommon. Blade edges are straight to slightly convex. Only a single and otherwise atypical example of a possible Chiricahua point is serrated. Basalt (n=7, 35%) and chert (n=7, 35%) are the most common material types for this style. Rhyolite is also relatively common, with five (25%) examples. Only one (5%) Chiricahua point is made from quartzite and one (5%) from siltstone.

The Chiricahua style is well dated for the southern Arizona region to the Middle Archaic period. A time range from 4800 to 4000 B.P. has been suggested (Mabry et al. 1998:79). At Locus L of the Arroyo site in the Picacho Reservoir study area (Bayham et al. 1986:226–227), a Chiricahua point was recovered from a stratigraphic context beneath a feature with a radiocarbon date of 4500 B.P. and above a stratum with a radiocarbon date of 4840 B.P. In a separate context at the site, a second Chiricahua point was found in a stratum that was associated with a radiocarbon date of 3910 B.P. These dates bracket the style to the time range from 4800 to 4000 B.P. and indicate that the style "may serve as diagnostic for the Middle Archaic in south-central Arizona" (Bayham et al. 1986:226).

A Chiricahua-style point was also recovered at a Middle Archaic site on the Santa Cruz River, where a hearth yielded a radiocarbon date of 4320 B.P. (Huckell 1996a:33). The site included numerous other artifacts, several hearths, and an immature bison skull, although Huckell cautions that the site had no "distinct cultural deposit." This date is consistent with the results from the Picacho Reservoir study.

Chiricahua types of points were first reported by Sayles and Antevs (1941) in their excavations along Cave Creek in southeastern Arizona, although at that time they did not use the phase name to refer specifically to this style of point. In some early reports the term *Chiricahua* is used to refer in general to the range of points found in Chiricahua phase components, and that usage could include Pinto and San Jose styles as well. In current usage the Chiricahua style refers specifically to concave-based, side-notched points (Bayham et al. 1986:226).

Table 9. Average Dimensions for Chiricahua Points in the Collection

Attribute	Range	Average	Sample Size
Length	26.2 mm–54.3 mm	35.0 mm	n=12
Neck Width	7.4 mm–18.9 mm	14.0 mm	n=20
Greatest Thickness	4.1 mm–8.8 mm	5.4 mm	n=20
Base Width	15.9 mm–22.9 mm	20.9 mm	n=13
Blade Width	14.0 mm–23.5 mm	17.9 mm	n=18

San Jose–Pinto A and San Jose–Pinto B

The definition of the San Jose–Pinto style has been the source of considerable debate since shortly after this style was first defined in 1935 (Campbell and Campbell 1935). As currently employed, points assigned to this style exhibit a considerable range of variation in appearance (Sliva 1999a:39). Consequently, many of the large points in the collection were assigned to this style, and it was necessary to further refine our understanding of the salient aspects of morphological variation for this type.

The systematics of the San Jose and Pinto styles has a long, complicated history (Mabry et al. 1998; Warren 1980). The San Jose style was initially defined for the San Jose Valley in New Mexico (Bryan and Toulouse 1943), and the Pinto style was first recognized in the Mojave Basin of southern California (Campbell and Campbell 1935). The two styles are similar and represent two ends of a spatial continuum, or cultural horizon, extending from western Texas across New Mexico and Arizona into southern California (Formby 1986; Irwin-Williams 1967; Rogers 1939). Irwin-Williams (1967) has demonstrated that the elements of this horizon extend well beyond styles of projectile points to include general similarities in subsistence practices, settlement systems, and demography. To avoid losing sight of this interregional pattern, researchers in Arizona have begun to combine the two style names in a single hyphenated term, as we have done in our nomenclature.

Although recognition of large-scale patterns is undeniably important, the considerable range of stylistic and technological variation that is grouped under the headings of the San Jose–Pinto style points has become a problem for chronological studies. For instance, researchers in the middle Gila Basin have quite good information on the age range of a style of point that lies toward the San Jose end of the continuum (Bayham et al. 1986), but such data cannot be applied to the age range of other varieties grouped under the term *San Jose–Pinto*. The chronological placement of each variant grouped under the term needs to be independently established for our local area.

The San Jose style was first defined for a collection of points found in surface collections of 12 lithic sites exposed in deflated sand dune areas in the San Jose Valley near Grants, New Mexico (Bryan and Toulouse 1943). The points had stems (or tangs) with concave sides and concave bases, and the blades were all heavily serrated. The edges of the stem had been smoothed by grinding (Bryan and Toulouse 1943:272–273). A dozen of the points were illustrated; one has an almost straight-sided stem, making it similar to some of the points illustrated by Campbell and Campbell (1935) for the Pinto Basin site in California. Leaf-shaped styles of points co-occur with the San Jose points but also appear in the following Ceramic period Lobo complex. Actually, some of the illustrated points attributed to the Lobo complex also fit the San Jose and the Pinto Basin style (Bryan and Toulouse 1943:273), so that both San Jose and leaf-shaped points appear to have been found in the Ceramic period sites, although this might have resulted from the mixing of Archaic and Ceramic period components.

Campbell and Campbell (1935) collected 160 Pinto points and 13 leaf-shaped points from the Pinto Basin "site," which was composed of a series of loci distributed on both banks for about 8 km (5 miles) along the Pinto Basin wash in the Mohave Desert, California (Campbell and Campbell 1935:26). The collections included grinding implements (slab metates), a full variety of flaked-stone tools and expedient flakes, and clusters of rocks that might have been hearths (Campbell and Campbell 1935:28). The 20 Pinto points illustrated in the text (Amsden 1935:47) include examples with straight stems, expanding stems, and several with only one shoulder; all the bases are either concave or straight, and the blades are either serrated or not serrated. The leaf-shaped points were not considered part of the Pinto style, although Rogers (1939) later included such points as one of his subcategories of Pinto.

Rogers (1939) defined five subcategories of styles to deal with the full variability he observed in Middle Archaic collections from southern California and Arizona. The predominant differences between his five subcategories of Pinto point styles are as follows:

1) shoulderless with concave base,
2) shouldered, straight-sided stem, concave to straight base,
3) shouldered, concave-sided or side-notched stem, deeply concave base,
4) shouldered, concave-sided or flared stem, straight base,
5) leaf-shaped or tapering stem, sometimes with small, concave base.

These subcategories nearly encompass the possible range of variability in shape for stone projectile points. Some examples of Type 3 (Formby 1986:107) resemble side-notched points rather than stemmed points (and come close to fitting the definition of Chiricahua points). The Type 1 subcategory includes everything from straight-sided to triangular points; what they have in common is the lack of a distinct shoulder separating the blade from the hafting element. The Type 5 category includes some points without a distinct shoulder (leaf-shaped) as well as points with a shoulder and a tapering stem; points in the latter category are similar to the long-tapered stemmed points of the Early Archaic period.

Harrington (1957) also defined five subcategories of Pinto points based on his work at the Stahl site in southern California, but his subcategories differ from those of Rogers. His subcategories include shoulderless, sloping shoulders, square shoulders, barbed shoulders, and one-shoulder style points (as cited in Formby 1986:100).

In discussing the evidence for the eastward extension of Rogers' (1939) Pinto-Gypsum complex, Formby (1986) illustrated more than 400 examples of Pinto and Gypsum points collected from sites in north-central Arizona, the Plains of San Augustin in New Mexico, and southwestern New Mexico. In all, his collections included 1,706 Pinto-style and 641 Gypsum-style points.

Formby's (1986) copious use of photographs helps illustrate the great diversity of styles that actually existed during the Middle Archaic period, and a data table reveals some interesting geographical differences in his data set. Gypsum points and all five of Rogers' subcategories of Pinto points occur in each of the three areas (Formby 1986:103), but Gypsum-style points are far more numerous (66%) in the collection from the Plains of San Augustine than those in either southwestern New Mexico (13%) or north-central Arizona (16%). In the two New Mexico collections, Type 3 (concave-sided stem with concave base) is the most abundant, followed by Type 1 (shoulderless); while in north-central Arizona, Type 1 (shoulderless) is more abundant, followed by Type 5 (leaf-shaped or tapering stem). Formby's and subsequent research clearly establishes the considerable variability in the styles of Middle Archaic points; the attempt to use one term (Pinto) to apply to five (and possibly even more) categories of styles is unfortunate. Each type could potentially have a very different temporal duration and possibly a different geographical distribution.

In at least some regions, Pinto and Gypsum styles are not contemporary and cannot be part of a single complex, despite Formby's demonstration that they tend to co-occur in surface deposits from parts of Arizona and New Mexico (1986). Some of the best evidence for this separation comes from stratified and well-dated cave deposits in the general area of the San Juan drainage on the northern Colorado Plateau (southern Utah). In Sudden Shelter Cave and Cowboy Cave on the northern Colorado Plateau, Pinto styles are dated between 8100 and 6700 B.P. and Gypsum points between 4600 and 3300 B.P. (Holmer 1980a:79, 83, 1980b:36–38); the styles are separated by a period of 1,500 years. (See the discussion of the dating of Gypsum styles below.) At the Dust Devil Cave in the same general part of the northern Colorado Plateau, Pinto-style points also appear at around 8800 to 8700 B.P. (Ambler 1996), much earlier than Gypsum-style points from cave deposits. Matson (1991) considers Pinto-style points to be an indicator of the Early Archaic period.

The situation is different in the Mojave Desert region of southern California, where the start of the Pinto style overlaps with the Mojave Lake tapering stemmed styles (about 8500 B.P.) and the end of the temporal distribution overlaps with the start of the Gypsum style (about 3900 B.P.). The Pinto style is dated as early as 8500 B.P. at the Rogers' Ridge site (Jenkins 1987), where it co-occurs with and eventually replaces Mojave short-stem styles of points. The Pinto style was still in use when the occupation of the Rogers' Ridge site terminated at around 5000 B.P. (Jenkins 1987:228), and a finely executed style of Pinto point co-occurs between 4600 and 3900 B.P. with Gypsum points at O'Malley's Shelter in southern Nevada (Jenkins and Warren 1984:48). By about 3500 B.P., the style was apparently no longer being made in the Mojave Desert, because it is absent from the deposits of that period in the Newberry Cave site (Jenkins and Warren 1984:47–48).

A similar pattern is found in the northern part of the Great Basin. There the Pinto style begins at around 8000 B.P. and overlaps with the first appearance of Gypsum points, persisting to 3000 B.P. at Hogup Cave and as late as 1000 B.P. at Danger Cave (Holmer 1980a:80).

In this study we have defined two subcategories that we call San Jose–Pinto A and San Jose–Pinto B. The type A variant is similar to Pinto points, and the maximum width of the blade is wider than the stem. The type B variant is similar to San Jose–style points, and the blade is narrower than or equal in size to the width of the stem. Mabry and colleagues (1998:68) make a similar distinction in their discussion of the San Jose complex. The San Jose–Pinto A style is part of the Pinto Basin complex and appears much earlier in the Great Basin (Mabry et al. 1998:59–61) than does the San Jose complex in New Mexico. In other words, the type B variant appears later than the type A variant, but both co-occur for about a thousand years (5500 to 4400 B.P.) during the latter part of the Middle Archaic. The San Jose–Pinto B style (San Jose–like) is securely dated in our study area while the San Jose–Pinto A style (Pinto Basin–like) is not.

The San Jose–Pinto A label applies to 12 of the 16 Pinto points illustrated by Campbell and Campbell (1935) from California, while the San Jose–Pinto B label applies to 10 of the 12 San Jose points illustrated by Bryan and Toulouse (1943:273) from New Mexico. Our San Jose–Pinto A is roughly equivalent to Rogers' Type 2 subcategory, and our San Jose–Pinto B is roughly equivalent to Rogers' Type 3 and possible 4 subcategories. Other of Rogers' subcategories are covered in our classification by styles with entirely different type names, such as Cortaro, Stemmed Teardrop, and Shouldered Teardrop.

The San Jose–Pinto B style of point was well dated within the local area as part of the Picacho Reservoir project (Bayham et al. 1986:68). An example of the style was found in the Middle Archaic components of the Buried Dune site, within a pit that contained charcoal with a calibrated radiocarbon date of 5430 to 4370 B.P. (one sigma) (Bayham et al. 1986:222). Four other examples of the San Jose–Pinto type B variant were recovered from other parts of the Buried Dune site. This component also included a triangular, concave-based point that in our classification would be assigned to the Cortaro style and would fit Rogers' Type 1 subcategory.

The dating of San Jose–Pinto A for our study area is much more problematical. To the east, our type A variant has been dated in New Mexico between 5900 and 4000 B.P. (Del Bene and Ford 1982; cited in Mabry et al. 1998:68), which is roughly equivalent to the date range of the variant B style as dated by the Picacho Reservoir project (Bayham et al. 1986). However, to the north (on the northern Colorado Plateau), the Pinto style, which is similar to our type A variant, is dated much earlier, to the period from 8100 to 6700 B.P., making it earlier than our type B variant. To the west (in the Mojave Desert and southern Nevada), projectile points similar to our type A variant persist from about 8000 B.P. to 4000 or 3500 B.P., making the style contemporary with the type B variant but beginning much earlier.

An important research objective for studies in the Middle Gila River valley is to obtain local dates for the age range of the type A variant of the San Jose–Pinto style. Investigators have developed three hypotheses for the duration of the type A variant: it persisted from about 6000 to 4000 B.P. and has a temporal assignment similar to the type B variant; it persisted from 8100 to 6700 B.P. and is earlier than the type B variant; or it persisted from 8000 to 4000 B.P. and is partially contemporary with the type B variant.

Some years ago, Warren (1980) raised the concern that the Pinto points found in the California deserts (Amsden 1935; Rogers 1939) might not be chronologically equivalent to similar-looking points found in the central and western Great Basin and suggested that perhaps points in the two areas should not be lumped into a single type (Vaughn and Warren 1987). Subsequently he and Vaughn demonstrated that significant differences existed in the populations of "Pinto"-looking points at the Awl site in the Mojave Desert and the Gatecliff site in Monitor Valley of the Great Basin. "Awl site points are thick and tend to have narrow sloping shoulders; . . . Gatecliff Split-stem points are thin and tend to have squared, wide shoulders" (Vaughn and Warren 1987:208). Moreover, raw material was not a factor in the morphological differences between the two populations (Vaughn and Warren 1987:210–211).

For a point style to be useful chronologically, the points in the type must consistently share a set of morphological attributes, and that set of shared attributes must have a continuous distribution in time as demonstrated through stratigraphic and chronological studies (Vaughn and Warren 1980:1987). Vaughn and Warren provide a concise summation of the principles of good systematics and of the discipline's use of styles as chronological markers. Because the populations of points in the Mojave Desert differ significantly from populations of points in the Great Basin (in short, the first condition does not hold), the two separate populations should not be expected to have the same temporal duration (Vaughn and Warren 1987; Warren 1980).

For this reason our emphasis is placed on styles that have been dated at sites within south-central Arizona; this approach increases the likelihood that we are dealing with the same populations of points, and therefore of styles. Use of chronological data from more distant regions increases the potential for drawing comparisons between substantially different populations, especially if the style has been loosely and poorly defined. Not surprisingly, chronology building for the Archaic period of south-central Arizona remains a major research priority.

The type A variant (Figure 4e) is more common in the study area than the type B variant, and 28 artifacts were classified as San Jose–Pinto A. Nearly 40% of the San Jose–Pinto A points are serrated. Basalt is the most common material type for this variant, with 19 (68%) examples. Single (4%) examples of obsidian and quartzite points were classified as San Jose–Pinto A. The remaining 7 (25%) points for this category are all chert.

Only 7 points (4 of which are serrated) were classified as San Jose–Pinto B (Figure 4f). Some of the type B examples are unusually long, including one measuring 66.3 millimeters in length. Interestingly, coarser-grained materials appear to have been preferred for type B points. Six (86%) of these points are made from basalt. The remaining point is quartzite (14%).

Table 10. Average Dimensions for San Jose–Pinto Type A Points in the Collection

Attribute	Range	Average	Sample Size
Length	20.0 mm–46.5 mm	32.6 mm	n=20
Neck Width	9.4 mm–16.7 mm	13.2 mm	n=28
Greatest Thickness	3.6 mm–8.2 mm	5.7 mm	n=28
Base Width	9.4 mm–20.1 mm	14.2 mm	n=27
Blade Width	13.9 mm–22.7 mm	17.3 mm	n=28

Table 11. Average Dimensions for San Jose–Pinto Type B Points in the Collection

Attribute	Range	Average	Sample Size
Length	31.1 mm–66.3 mm	39.9 mm	n=7
Neck Width	11.1 mm–17.3 mm	12.9 mm	n=7
Greatest Thickness	3.6 mm–8.1 mm	5.2 mm	n=7
Base Width	12.5 mm–18.7 mm	15.1 mm	n=6
Blade Width	14.0 mm–19.2 mm	17.0 mm	n=7

Gypsum

These distinctive projectile points have short stems that contract, with abrupt shoulders (Figure 4g). Only 9 artifacts were classified as this type. A single point is serrated, and this example is also otherwise atypical. Given the small sample size, Gypsum points are made from a surprising diversity of materials. Basalt and chert are the most common materials, with 3 (33%) examples each. Single examples (11%) of dacite, quartz, and rhyolite points were classified as Gypsum style.

In the Sonoran Desert, the Gypsum Cave style is generally assigned to the Middle Archaic period because it has frequently been found with Pinto-style points (Formby 1986; Huckell 1984:131; Mabry et al. 1998:144). However, a growing body of dates from surrounding regions suggests that this may instead be a Late Archaic or perhaps a transitional style, at least in some parts of the Southwest. Huckell (1996b) cites a series of sources suggesting that Gypsum Cave-style points date from 4400 to 2100 B.P., and Mabry (1998:144) suggests a range of 4500 to 1500 B.P., both of which include part of the Late Archaic period.

Thomas (1981:35) reviews the general style of Gypsum Cave points (which he calls "Gatecliff contracting stem" in his classification). The initial assignment (Harrington 1933) of the style to the Paleo-Indian period (based on radiocarbon dating of dung) was incorrect, because wooden artifacts in Gypsum Cave have been dated between 3000 and 2000 B.P. (Holmer 1980b:36; Thomas 1981:35). In the eastern Great Basin at the O'Malley Shelter, the style falls in the Middle to Late Archaic time range (4700 to 3100 B.P.), but it has also been found at sites dating in the Current Era, ranging from 1230 to 600 B.P. (Thomas 1981:35–36).

On the northern Colorado Plateau in Utah, the style is dated from 4600 B.P. (at Sudden Shelter Cave) to 1500 B.P. (at Cowboy Cave), and it actually reaches its maximum abundance at the end of this time range (Holmer 1980a, 1980b). At the Sudden Shelter site, archaeologists documented a continuous stratigraphic sequence from 8000 B.P. to 3000 B.P. (Jennings et al. 1980:20–21); the Gypsum style first appears in the sequence around 4600 B.P., although it does not become abundant until after 3500 B.P. (Holmer 1980a:79–83). The Sudden Shelter sequence ends at 3000 B.P. and cannot be used to establish the end date for the style, but in the Cowboy Cave sequence, which continues to about 1500 B.P., the Gypsum style is abundant in strata at 1900 B.P. and is absent from strata dating around 1600 to 1500 B.P. A hiatus in the Cowboy Cave sequence starting at 6400 B.P. and continuing at least until 4500 B.P. (if not later) prevents the use of the site to establish the initial date for the style (Holmer 1980b:31–38; Jennings et al. 1980:27–29).

The date range for the Gypsum-style point in the Sonoran Desert is tentatively set at 4700 to 2600 B.P., although the limited local evidence suggests that the style tends to co-occur with Middle Archaic points more regularly than with Late Archaic points. It occurs in Ventana Cave in association with Pinto-style points (Haury 1950). Gypsum Cave points occur at one site in the Rosemont study area (Huckell 1984:128–135) along with both Middle (San Jose–Pinto) and Late (San Pedro) Archaic points, and in the Picacho Reservoir area, the style was found in surface collections along with Middle through Late Archaic styles (Bayham et al. 1986:422–427).

An important research objective for southern Arizona Archaic studies is to date the Gypsum Cave style and determine its relative association with other point styles in sites within the region. Until the chronological placement of this style is determined for the local region, researchers should recognize that in surrounding regions this style occurs in Late Archaic as well as Middle Archaic contexts, and thus should not be treated as a marker unique to the Middle Archaic period.

Thomas (1981:36–37) cautions that the point series have very different cultural histories in the western and eastern parts of the Great Basin and that quite similar morphological forms have very different temporal duration in the two areas. This potentially applies to the Archaic sequences of the Sonoran Desert in relationship to those of the Great Basin or Colorado Plateau regions as well. Archaeologists have as yet established no good independent sequence of radiocarbon dates for the Gypsum style here in the southern desert, and as a result we are forced to apply the dates for the type available from the surrounding regions. Research that can generate a better chronology is therefore needed.

Table 12. Average Dimensions for Gypsum Points in the Collection

Attribute	Range	Average	Sample Size
Length	27.3 mm–43.5 mm	34.5 mm	n=8
Neck Width	9.5 mm–14.1 mm	11.5 mm	n=9
Greatest Thickness	4.6 mm–7.6 mm	6.0 mm	n=9
Base Width	2.3 mm–12.5 mm	5.9 mm	n=9
Blade Width	17.2 mm–25.7 mm	21.0 mm	n=9

Cortaro

These large triangular points lack notching or a stem (Figure 4h). Only 14 projectile points were classified as Cortaro points. Points that lack notching or stems, however, were commonly identified in the small point collection. In contrast to many other large point styles, basalt is uncommon for Cortaro points: only a single (7%) Cortaro point is made from basalt. Chert is by far the most common material, with 10 (71%) examples. One (7%) example is chalcedony, and 2 (14%) are rhyolite.

Sliva (1999a:40) observes that this type exhibits a "great deal of variation in both morphology and flaking execution, ranging from thin, symmetrical, pressure-flaked points to thick, blocky, irregular percussion-flaked ones—often at the same site." This point style may be difficult to distinguish from nearly completed preforms, which could at least partially account for the apparent range of variation in appearance and manufacturing technique for this style.

Blade edges are straight to slightly convex, and base treatment varies from concave to convex. The presence of isolated masses of stone caused by step fractures or other factors that precluded further thinning were employed to distinguish preforms from completed unnotched projectile points. None of the Cortaro points in the collection are serrated.

The Cortaro-style point has a fairly limited spatial distribution, although not as limited as claimed by researchers in the Hohokam area (e.g. Lorentzen1998:147). It is well documented in the area to the south of the Gila River, but also occurs in sites in pre-ceramic sites in the Mogollon region (Matson 1991:282–283). It was first defined by Roth and site included a Late Archaic component with San Pedro and Cienega points; although investigators could not establish a good chronological determination for the Cortaro style, they concluded that it seemed to be earlier than the other materials (Huckell 1995:139). The assignment of the Cortaro style to a Middle Archaic date of 4500 to 4000 B.P. is based on the

Table 13. Average Dimensions for Cortaro Points in the Collection

Attribute	Range	Average	Sample Size
Length	37.2 mm–55 mm	47.6 mm	n=10
Neck Width	15.3 mm–33.6 mm	24.5 mm	n=12
Greatest Thickness	3.8 mm–7.8 mm	6.3 mm	n=14
Base Width	12.7 mm–28.2 mm	21.4 mm	n=13
Blade Width	15.8 mm–34.9 mm	25 mm	n=13

excavation of the site of Los Pozos on the floodplain of the Santa Cruz River (Gregory 1999).

A Cortaro-style point was also found in the Middle Archaic stratum of the Buried Dune site (about 4300 B.P.) in association with San Jose–Pinto points (Bayham et al. 1986:422–427), although the style had yet to be given a name.

Although the Cortero style is well dated to the Middle Archaic, it is nonetheless the case that it tends to occur in low frequencies but with some regularity in association with Cienega and San Pedro styles (Early Agricultural Period) styles at a number of sites, such as the Santa Cruz Bend and Stone Pipe sites (Mabry et al. 1997) in the Tucson Basin and the Donaldson site (Huckell 1995:51–54) farther east. It also occurs in the Central Mountains of Arizona in association with Maize and Cienega and San Pedro points at Tularosa Cave and O-Block Caves (Matson 1991:282-283; 289). The Cortero style may have persisted from the Middle Archaic into the Early Agricultural Period, which makes it quite important as evidence of continuity between the two periods in the Sonoran desert area at least.

Table 14. Average Dimensions for Shouldered Teardrop Points in the Collection

Attribute	Range	Average	Sample Size
Length	24.8 mm–41.3 mm	34.5 mm	n=8
Neck Width	9.8 mm– 16.5 mm	11.7 mm	n=9
Greatest Thickness	3.3 mm–5.9 mm	4.7 mm	n=9
Base Width	6.7 mm–13.7 mm	10.0 mm	n=9
Blade Width	14.4 mm–24.1 mm	18.0 mm	n=9

Teardrop Style

Teardrop-shaped points (Figures 5a & 5b) from the middle Gila River area are similar to leaf-shaped points in the Mojave Desert (Campbell and Campbell 1935; Jenkins 1987) and lanceolate or leaf-shaped styles in the Great Basin (Holmer 1980a), where they are associated with Middle Archaic contexts. Leaf-shaped points have been found in association with Pinto points in surface collections at the Pinto Basin site in the Mojave Desert (Campbell and Campbell

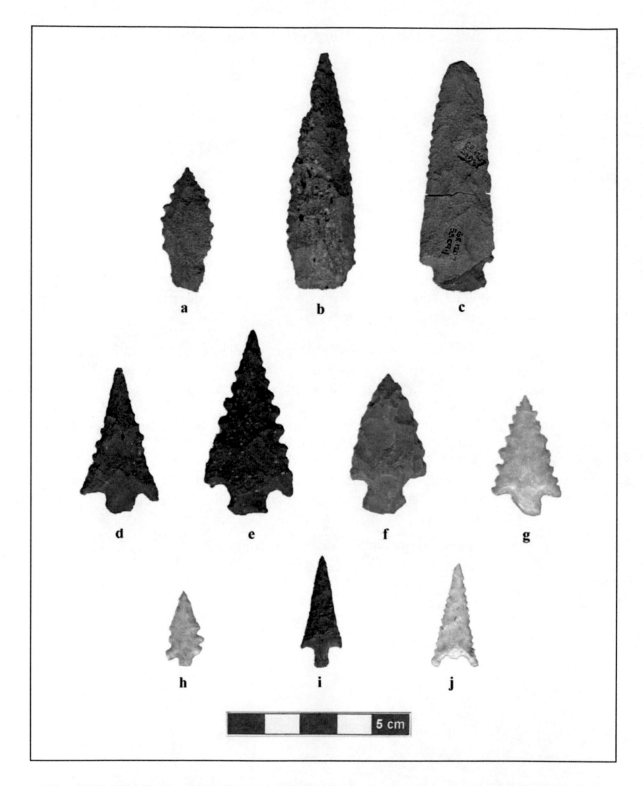

Figure 5. Middle Archaic, Late Archaic, Early Agricultural and Hohokam Point Styles from the Gila River Indian Community: a) Shouldered Teardrop; b) Stemmed Teardrop; c) San Pedro; d) Cienega Flared; e) Cienega Long; f) Cienega Short; g) Cienega Stemmed; h) Stemmed Barbed; i) Stemmed Shouldered; j) Stemmed Tanged

Table 15. Average Dimensions for Stemmed Teardrop Points in the Collection

Attribute	Range	Average	Sample Size
Length	31.4 mm–68.1 mm	49.9 mm	n=12
Neck Width	9.0 mm–17.2 mm	12.4 mm	n=12
Greatest Thickness	5.0 mm–8.4 mm	6.5 mm	n=12
Base Width	6.7 mm–15.2 mm	10.1 mm	n=11
Blade Width	16.0 mm–23.7 mm	19.1 mm	n=12

1935). At the Rodgers Ridge site, they occur in context with both Short-Stemmed Mojave Lake and Pinto styles in an occupation transitional between the Early and Middle Archaic periods, dated to 8400 and 8000 B.P. (Jenkins 1987:228–229).

Lanceolate-style points were recovered at Sudden Shelter Cave in the Great Basin in strata dating to the period 4700 to 3700 B.P. (Holmer 1980a:83) and do not occur in strata representing the final 350 years of the cave's occupation. In the Sudden Shelter Cave, these points occur considerably later than the Pinto point styles. However, Willow Leaf points very similar in style to the lanceolates of Sudden Shelter Cave (Holmer 1980a:83) are dated at the O'Malley Shelter (Fowler et al. 1973) from 5500 B.P. to the Fremont phase.

The earliest absolute date for teardrop-style points is about 8400 B.P. in the Mojave Desert, and they are present at least by 5500 B.P. in the Great Basin. Despite this considerable antiquity, some teardrop-style points continue into the Ceramic period in parts of the Great Basin. Brew and Huckell (1987:171) suggest that leaf-shaped bifaces, some of which are very similar in appearance to the teardrop-style projectile points, were produced during the early portion of the Historic period in the Sonoran Desert.

Four teardrop- or leaf-shaped points were recovered from Archaic sites in the Picacho Reservoir area (Bayham et al. 1986). Two of these were associated with the Arroyo site dating to the Middle Archaic period, but one was recovered from the surface (Bayham et al. 1986:236) and the other from water-redeposited strata in Locus A of the site (Bayham et al. 1986:225). A third point (Bayham et al. 1986:235) was recovered from the surface of a site that also included a Pinto point, suggesting a Middle Archaic context as well. The fourth point (Bayham et al. 1986:238) was recovered from a shallow deposit that could not be dated. Although these four leaf-shaped points were collected from contexts with poor temporal control, they appear to be associated with Middle Archaic deposits, which is consistent with the dating of the style in the Great Basin and Mojave Desert areas.

For the purposes of research in the middle Gila River basin, the style is assigned to the Middle Archaic period and the early part of the Late Archaic period, with the recognition that it could persist into the Ceramic period, and might appear by 8400 B.P. in Early Archaic period contexts. Consequently, the age range suggested here is a very tentative chronological assignment open to considerable revision.

Teardrop-style points are not illustrated in the reports for the Rosemont (Huckell 1984), Santa Cruz Flats (Halbirt and Henderson 1993), Middle Santa Cruz Valley (Mabry 1998), and Los Pozos (Gregory 1999) investigations. Some bifaces that are unsuitable for use as projectile points also have a lanceolate or teardrop form, and analysts must be careful to maintain the distinction between projectile points and bifacial knives. In other studies, potential examples of this point style might have been grouped with bifaces and consequently not recognized as projectile points. However, this issue is unlikely to fully account for the apparent absence of teardrop-shaped projectile points, and they are probably uncommon in these areas.

Two variants of teardrop-style points (shouldered and stemmed) were defined for this analysis. Shouldered Teardrop points have abrupt shoulders, convex blade margins, and a straight to contracting stem (Figure 5a). These points are frequently serrated; 5 (56%) of 9 examples of this type have this form of edge treatment. Basalt is the most common material, with 6 (67%) of these points made from basalt. Individual (11%) examples of rhyolite, chert, and obsidian points were also classified as this style.

Stemmed Teardrop points are similar to Shouldered Teardrop points, except that they have sloping shoulders, and the stems are shorter or not as distinct from the blade (Figure 5b). Stemmed Teardrop points are also generally serrated, with 8 (67%) of the 12 examples having this form of edge treatment. In some instances, these two variants are difficult to distinguish, as the shoulder treatment often varies between blade margins. Basalt accounts for 9 (75%) of the Stemmed Teardrop points. Single examples (8%) of meta-basalt, quartzite, and rhyolite were also identified.

Late Archaic/Early Formative Styles

The typology includes five different styles (four being variants of Cienega points) assigned to the Late Archaic or Early Formative periods. A total of 62 points in the collection was assigned to these styles, which are thought to date between roughly 1200 B.C. and A.D. 550.

San Pedro

These large projectile points have corner notching, expanding stems that are almost as wide as the blade, straight to slightly convex bases, and generally straight blade margins (Figure 5c). This style is widely distributed across Arizona (Slaughter et al. 1992:81). These projectile points are generally large, and in some instances they may have been used as hafted knives rather than exclusively as projectile points. The San Pedro points analyzed here, however, largely lack evidence of use; only a single example has macroscopic usewear. San Pedro points are relatively common in the collection, with 27 examples of this style. Serration is relatively rare; 75 percent of the San Pedro points lack this form of edge treatment.

Material types for San Pedro points vary somewhat from other large points. In contrast to all other styles, rhyolite is the most common material, with 9 (33%) examples. Chert is the next most common: 8 (30%) of the San Pedro points are made from this material.

Four (14%) of the points are basalt, three (11%) are quartzite, and single examples (4%) are meta-basalt, quartz, and siltstone.

The greater tendency for San Pedro points to be made from rhyolite is probably, in part, a result of raw material constraints combined with the generally large size of these points. This factor, however, does not appear to fully account for the higher proportion of rhyolite San Pedro points, because other styles that are generally long are not more frequently made from this material. For example, Stemmed Teardrop points are longer on average than San Pedro points, and the most common material for these points is basalt (75%). At least two other factors could account for the variation. First, rhyolite points may have been transported to the area as finished products. This possibility is supported by the low incidence of rhyolite in the point collection. Second, trade networks or possibly mobility patterns may have differed during the Late Archaic and Early Agricultural periods from the Middle Archaic. This possibility is supported by the observation that rhyolite was also frequently used for another Late Archaic style (Cienega Long). These three possibilities are not mutually exclusive, and all three may have occurred.

Table 16. Average Dimensions for San Pedro Points in the Collection

Attribute	Range	Average	Sample Size
Length	17.7 mm – 63.7 mm	42.0 mm	n=17
Neck Width	10.7 mm – 20.3 mm	13.8 mm	n=27
Greatest Thickness	4.5 mm – 9.0 mm	6.3 mm	n=27
Base Width	10.3 mm – 23.8 mm	15.1 mm	n=26
Blade Width	15.1 mm – 31.0 mm	21.6 mm	n=26

San Pedro points appear with the start of the Late Archaic period, are the diagnostic point type for the San Pedro phase, and persist into the following Cienega phase (Huckell 1995:118–119; Mabry et al. 1997:208–209). The style was first recorded in southern Arizona (Sayles and Antevs 1941), where it is well represented, but the distribution does extend northward into Colorado and northwestern New Mexico, eastward into Texas, and southward into Mexico (Mabry et al. 1997:209).

The style is well dated in a number of sites in southern Arizona, as shown below:

Site Name (Reference)	Date Range	Sample Size
Milagro (Huckell 1995:139)	3200–3000 B.P.	no count
Fairbanks (Huckell 1995:138)	2500–2300 B.P.	no count
Coffee Camp (Halbirt and Henderson 1993)	2250–1800 B.P.	17 points
Santa Cruz Bend (Mabry 1998:311)	2700–2150 B.P.	4 points
Stone Pipe (Mabry 1998:334)	2350–2200 B.P.	3 points

The Coffee Camp site is the closest of these sites to the Gila River, being located on the Santa Cruz flats only about 44.8 km (28 miles) south. During the latter portion of the period in which these points were made, they co-occur with Cienega-style points. Sliva (1999b) suggests the San Pedro style may have persisted into the Agua Caliente phase of the Early Ceramic period (A.D. 150 to 650).

The San Pedro style appeared earliest in the Sonoran and Chihuahuan deserts, and moved gradually northward along with maize agriculture, abruptly replacing the Gypsum style in the more northerly regions. Starting by 3200 B.P. in the Sonoran and Chihuahuan deserts (Huckell 1995:139), the point style and maize had spread to the central mountains of the Mogollon region by 2800 B.P. Interestingly, Cienega points occur with San Pedro points in these sites in the central mountains (Matson 1991:282–288), and 2800 B.P. is when Cienega points also appear in the Sonoran Desert (Gregory 2001:253).

Maize and the associated point styles did not make it to the Colorado Plateau until 2500 B.P. The Basketmaker II style points of the Colorado Plateau are essentially identical to San Pedro style points, and have been given different names only because researchers were unaware of the data from other regions (Matson 1991). San Pedro/Basketmaker II style points appear along with maize on the Colorado Plateau by 2500 B.P. This is also the time when maize and San Pedro points show up in the western Sonoran Desert in the area around Kingman (Matson 1991:116–117). The gradual northward movement of the San Pedro style in association with maize, and sometimes with Cienega style points, is documented in the following list of sites:

Site Name (Reference)	Date Range
Central Mountains (San Pedro and Cienega)	
Cordova Cave (Matson 1991:288)	2800 B.P.
U-Block Cave (Matson 1991:288)	2780 B.P.
Tularosa Cave (Matson 1991:282)	2500–2000 B.P.
Colorado Plateau (San Pedro/Basketmaker II)	
Three Fir Shelter (Matson 1991:116–117)	2500–2200 B.P.
Kinboko Caves (Matson 1991:116–117)	2500 B.P.
White Dog Cave (Matson 1991:116–117)	2300–2100 B.P.
AZ Q:7:22 (ASM) (Matson 1991:121–122)	2400–2100 B.P.
Western Sonoran Desert	
Big Horn Cave (Matson 1991:172)	2500 B.P.

Cienega Styles

The Cienega style was defined by Huckell (1988) and is well dated at several Early Agricultural period sites in southern Arizona (Huckell 1995; Mabry 1998). The date range for the Cienega phase is given by Huckell (1995:118–119) as 2450 B.P. to about 1850 B.P. More recently, Mabry (1998:18) has moved the beginning of the phase back to 2700 B.P. Age estimate ranges (corrected radiocarbon dates) for four Cienega phase components and the number of Cienega points recovered from those deposits are as follows:

Site Name (Reference)	**Date Range**	**Sample Size**
Donaldson (Huckell 1995:51–54)	2600–2300 B.P.	27 points
Santa Cruz Bend (Mabry 1998:311)	2700–2150 B.P.	8 points
Stone Pipe (Mabry 1998:334)	2350–2200 B.P.	8 points
Coffee Camp (Halbirt and Henderson 1993)	2250–1850 B.P.	2 points

One of the perplexing research issues for the Early Agricultural period of southern Arizona is that no evidence for the use of cultigens exists at Coffee Camp despite the abundance of such evidence from contemporary sites a relatively short distance upstream in the Santa Cruz Valley. Coffee Camp also has the latest ranges of dates.

Cienega point styles co-occur quite consistently with San Pedro styles, while San Pedro styles often occur in the absence of Cienega points. The pattern of San Pedro points in association with Cienega points is found at Coffee Camp (Halbirt and Henderson 1993:76–78), the Donaldson and Los Ojitos sites (Huckell 1995:51–70), the Split Ridge site (Huckell 1984:163–168), and the Santa Cruz Bend and Stone Pipe sites (Mabry 1998:311, 334).

Four variants of the Cienega style have recently been suggested (Sliva 1999b). These styles appear to have made during different periods of time and have different raw material frequencies; some may have been the first local points to be used on arrows as opposed to atlatl darts.

Cienega Flared

These large corner-notched projectile points have expanding stems, concave blade margins, tapered tips, barbed shoulders, and serration (Figure 5d). Only a single example of this style of point was identified in the collection, and it has only moderately concave blade margins. Although this style nearly absent from the study area, the type is generally associated with Cienega phase agricultural sites in floodplain settings (Sliva 1999b:343) and most of the surveyed area is outside this setting. Sliva suggests that these points were restricted to the latter portion of the Cienega phase (roughly 2700 to 1800 B.P.). The single possible Cienega Flared point in the collection is made from rhyolite.

Table 17. Average Dimensions for Cienega Flared Points in the Collection

Attribute	Range	Average	Sample Size
Length	40.8 mm	40.8 mm	n=1
Neck Width	8.5 mm	8.5 mm	n=1
Greatest Thickness	5.1 mm	5.1 mm	n=1
Base Width	8.5 mm	8.5 mm	n=1
Blade Width	22.0 mm	22.0 mm	n=1

Cienega Long

These points have straight blade margins, long expanding tangs, and barbed shoulders (Figure 5e). This type is similar to Cienega Short but has a greater length. Sliva (2001:106) suggests that these points were made throughout the Cienega phase, roughly between 2700 and 1800 B.P. These points are relatively common, with 15 points assigned to this style. Only one of these points is serrated. Seven (47%) points are basalt. The next most common material is rhyolite, with five (33%) examples. Two (13%) of the Cienega Long points are chert. A single (7%) siltstone example is also present in the collection.

Table 18. Average Dimensions for Cienega Long Points in the Collection

Attribute	Range	Average	Sample Size
Length	33.7 mm – 52.5 mm	43.7 mm	n= 8
Neck Width	6.8 mm – 13.2 mm	9.6 mm	n=15
Greatest Thickness	4.3 mm – 8.0 mm	4.4 mm	n=15
Base Width	9.7 mm – 15.3 mm	12.5 mm	n=12
Blade Width	17.1 mm – 25.1 mm	19.8 mm	n=14

Cienega Short

These projectile points are smaller but otherwise similar in appearance to Cienega Long. They have straight blade margins, long expanding tangs, and barbed shoulders (Figure 5f). Sliva (2001:106) argues that these points date primarily to the latter portion of the Cienega phase (roughly 2300 to 1800 B.P.). Twelve examples of Cienega Short points were identified in the collection, a single example of which is serrated. A discriminate analysis performed by Sliva (1999b) suggests that most Cienega Short points fall into the size range of arrow projectile tips, and this style may be associated with the introduction of bow-and-arrow technology in the region.

Interestingly, Cienega Long and Cienega Short points appear to vary significantly (Chi-square probability = 0.01) in material types (see Table 2). In contrast to the tendency for Cienega Long to be basalt or rhyolite, chert is the most common material for Cienega Short points, with eight (67%) examples. Only two (17%) points are basalt, and individual examples (8%) of obsidian and rhyolite points are present. Although the relatively small sample sizes and associated low expected frequencies are problematical, the available data support the suggestion by Sliva (1999b:346) that Cienega Short points are a distinct type that primarily are not reworked Cienega Long points. Although not parsimonious, it is also possible that larger Cienega points of certain material types may have broken more often and been reworked into Cienega Short points. However, this latter possibility does not appear to be well supported by the data, because the median length for chert points is actually somewhat greater than that of basalt.

Table 19. Average Dimensions for Cienega Short Points in the Collection

Attribute	Range	Average	Sample Size
Length	19.6 mm – 30.9 mm	25.8 mm	n=8
Neck Width	5.7 mm – 13.3 mm	8.8 mm	n=12
Greatest Thickness	3.4 mm – 7.3 mm	5.2 mm	n=12
Base Width	6.6 mm – 15.5 mm	10.2 mm	n=9
Blade Width	12.2 mm – 23.2 mm	17.8 mm	n=12

Cienega Stemmed

These points differ from other Cienega styles in that they have straight to slightly contracting stems (Figure 5g). They are also much more commonly serrated than other Cienega styles; six of the seven examples in the collection have this form of edge treatment. Sliva (1999b) suggests that these points date between 2500 to 1400 B.P. and also argues that most Cienega Stemmed points are the size of arrow projectile tips. Three (43%) Cienega Stemmed points are basalt, two (29%) are chert, and single examples (14%) of obsidian and rhyolite are present.

Table 20. Average Dimensions for Cienega Stemmed Points in the Collection

Attribute	Range	Average	Sample Size
Length	24.2 mm – 33.4 mm	31.9 mm	n=6
Neck Width	5.0 mm – 10.8 mm	8.5 mm	n=7
Greatest Thickness	2.7 mm – 5.4 mm	4.7 mm	n=7
Base Width	6.9 mm – 10.9 mm	9.0 mm	n=6
Blade Width	12.8 mm – 20.5 mm	18.0 mm	n=7

CHAPTER 3

SMALL PROJECTILE POINT COMPLEX

Small projectile points or preforms are substantially more common than large projectile points. In total, 687 artifacts were thought to be small projectile points or small point preforms. The classification of small point styles that was developed following Sliva (1997) is presented in Table 21. Projectile points that lack notching or a stem dominate the small point complex. Side-notched point types are somewhat common, but corner-notched styles are not included. Stemmed points also appear to be uncommon in the small point collection.

Most previous analyses of point collections from the Hohokam area have tended to focus on only a few point attributes (for example, the presence or absence of notching) within given samples. Attention is sometimes given to the perceived "quality" of the workmanship as well. Sayles (Gladwin et al. 1965[1937]) was one of the first researchers to classify Hohokam points recovered from initial excavations at Snaketown. His system included only seven classes that are based on differences in morphology and perceived temporal association. Subsequent researchers did not systematically employ this system.

Crabtree (1973) completed one of the first detailed technological analyses of Hohokam points. The main intent of his analysis was the identification of specific manufacturing techniques employed and consideration of the craftsmanship quality. He argued that the skill necessary to produce some point styles suggests specialization by individuals in the production of projectile points. Researchers also failed to adopt the classification system proposed by Crabtree.

Subsequent typologies of Hohokam projectile points have been largely descriptive (for example, Bernard-Shaw 1988; Hoffman 1988; Montero 1993; Peterson 1994; Rozen 1984), and the temporal systematics of Hohokam points have received less attention (Hoffman 1997; Sliva 1997). For example, Bernard-Shaw (1988) employed a taxonomic system to classify the Sedentary to Classic period points from Las Colinas. This system employed the presence or absence of serration, notches, tangs, and basal concavity to differentiate the points. In addition, a separate style was employed for points that were thought to have been reworked.

In general, Hohokam collections are classified into categories based on ad hoc criteria such as the presence or absence of serration, with little or no attempt to create temporally sensitive types. Consequently, extremely little consistency exists among classification systems employed by previous researchers to type Hohokam projectile points. Peterson (1994:103) has noted that "many studies have dealt with relatively small collections from single-component sites." This factor, combined with the availability of better age estimates

Table 21. Definitions of Small (Ceramic Period) Point Styles Used in This Volume

Stemmed Barbed: narrow triangular blade with pairs of barbs at the base, slightly expanding stem, convex base.

Stemmed Shouldered: long triangular blade, narrow slightly contracting stem, abrupt shoulders.

Stemmed Tanged: long triangular blade, contracting stem, barbed shoulders.

Narrow Side-Notched: narrow and deep side notches near the lower one-third of the point, thin triangular blades, straight blade margins, and straight to slightly concave base.

Wide Side-Notched: wide side notches near the lower one-third of the point, thick triangular blade, straight to slightly concave base.

Intermediate Side-Notched: triangular blade, intermediate width side notches near the lower one-third of the point, straight to slightly concave base.

Upper Side-Notched: side-notched above the midpoint, triangular blade, straight to slightly concave base.

Middle Side-Notched: side-notched near the midpoint, triangular blade, straight to slightly concave base.

Flanged: lacks notching or stem, long triangular blade, flanged base, haft element wider than the blade.

Bulbous Base: lacks notching or stem, short narrow blade, irregular flanged base, irregular concave base.

Concave Blade: lacks notching or stem, serrated, straight to slightly concave base, concave blade margins.

Straight Blade Serrated: lacks notching or stem, serrated, v-shaped base.

Concave Base Triangular: lacks notching or stem, straight blade margins, deeply concave crescent-shaped base.

Thin Triangular: lacks notching or stem, uniformly thin, straight to slightly concave base.

Long Triangular: lacks notching or stem, straight blade margins, length-to-width ratio roughly 3:1.

Straight Base Triangular: lacks notching or stem, straight to slightly concave base, straight blade margins.

U-shaped Base Triangular: lacks notching or stem, deeply concave u-shaped base, straight blade margins.

Eccentric: Idiosyncratic points with deeply serrated or barbed blade margins.

---

from other lines of evidence (particularly ceramics), probably accounts for the general lack of emphasis placed on the temporal sequencing of Hohokam point collections. In addition, the Hohokam appear to have produced more than one point style at a given moment in time, which complicates the creation of temporally relevant types. Some previous attempts to seriate Hohokam points have concluded that morphological changes through time were poorly defined (Peterson 1994:112).

The typology developed by Hoffman (1997) for the classification of Hohokam points was primarily concerned with synchronic rather than diachronic variation among Hohokam projectile points, and thus is of limited utility for the present analysis. His intent was to "address questions about the ethnic and/or linguistic diversity of regional Hohokam populations, and their potential organization into one or more alliances" (Hoffman 1997:iii). His analysis employed collections from three geographical areas, including the middle Gila River (Snaketown collections), the Lower Salt River, and the Gila Bend area. "Most of the points were recovered in mortuary contexts, although a few points associated with domestic and trash contexts are also included" (Hoffman 1997:162). His focus on points from mortuary contexts creates additional problems, which will be discussed further below, for comparisons with the current study. Hoffman identified quantitative variation among these three geographical areas that he interpreted as evidence for social variation among them.

Recently, Justice reviewed much of the Southwestern research to date and attempted to define projectile point styles based on both regional and temporal variation. He defines three style "clusters" that occur on the middle Gila during the Ceramic period, including the "Western Triangular Cluster," the "Snaketown Cluster," and "Pueblo Side- Notched Cluster" (Justice 2002). He assumes a strict relationship existed between the styles he defines and prehistoric cultures. However, examples of virtually all of the small point styles he defines for the entire Southwestern region are present among the large collection of points considered here, while at the same time several styles he suggests typify the Hohokam are extremely rare in the GRIC-CRMP collection. In addition, styles in his typology are not systematically differentiated, which frustrates comparisons with the typology presented here.

A further factor complicating comparisons with the various samples considered by previous Hohokam researchers is that these collections are generally derived from a variety of archaeological contexts, whereas the present study is based exclusively on surface context materials. In particular, previous analyses of large Hohokam collections include substantial numbers of points from mortuary contexts, whereas these contexts are largely not represented in the collection considered here. Points from burial contexts frequently differ markedly from those recovered in other contexts, and individual interments may be associated with large numbers of highly similar projectile points (for example, Loendorf 1997; McGregor 1943; Peterson 1994; Whittaker 1987). This variation has been variously interpreted (for example, the points from mortuary contexts are sometimes assumed to be too large or fragile for use), but whatever its source, failure to control for recovery context affects comparisons across time and space to the extent that sampled contexts are not uniformly distributed across these dimensions.

Temporal Estimates

Point styles discussed in the following sections are thought to encompass the period between roughly A.D. 750 until stone points were last made locally sometime shortly after the end of the nineteenth century (Russell 1908). Early Formative (roughly A.D. 1150 to A.D. 650) styles are not currently differentiated from Late Archaic/Early Agricultural styles (roughly 1500 B.C. to A.D. 1/150), which were discussed in previous sections. No styles are yet defined for the Pioneer period between roughly A.D. 650 to 750.

Only three types, all of which are stemmed, are currently thought to be distinctive Colonial Period (roughly A.D. 750 to 950) styles. Each of these styles exhibits narrow stems that may have been intended to split the arrow shaft on impact, thus loosening the point. Stemmed projectile points are uncommon in small point collection, and only 12 projectile points were assigned to these three styles. The apparently small number of Colonial period points does not accurately reflect the intensity of Hohokam use of the study area during this time period; it appears that certain styles that Sliva (1997) suggests are from the Sedentary period were actually first manufactured prior to this time. Additional research, particularly samples of projectile points from excavated Colonial period contexts, is necessary to resolve these issues.

Four styles in the Sliva typology are suggested to be from the Sedentary period (roughly A.D. 950 to 1150); three of these styles are side-notched. The intermediate side-notched style from this period is not systematically differentiated from the Late Classic Side-Notched style in the Sliva typology. Consequently, it was necessary to combine these styles, and further research is necessary to define variation between Sedentary and Classic period side-notched styles. Based on a subjective assessment of the Sliva styles, 92 of the points in the assemblage may have been made during the Sedentary period.

Not surprisingly, Classic period points (roughly A.D. 1150 to 1450) appear to be common based on the Sliva types, with 134 examples. The Sliva typology includes nine types that may have been produced most commonly during this period.

Projectile point morphology after the Classic period, from roughly A.D. 1450 until the early twentieth century, is still poorly understood. Preliminary consideration of projectile points collected from known Protohistoric/Historic sites in the study area suggests that small unnotched projectile points (with or without serration) are by far the most common type. For example, 117 projectile points were collected from GR-909, a large Protohistoric/Historic period site on the south bank of the Gila River (Randolph et al. 2002), and all 87 of the small points that could be typed lacked notches.

Although relatively little research has been done (Gilpin and Phillips 1998:91), Protohistoric projectile points attributed to the O'odham are generally suggested to be small triangular points that lack notches (Brew and Huckell 1987:171; Gilpin and Phillips 1998; Haury 1950; Rosenthal et al. 1978). Haury (1950:268), for example, suggests a pattern at Ventana Cave where unnotched points occurred only sporadically prior to the appearance of ceramics, but were common afterward until intensive use of the cave stopped. Further, Haury (1950:274) describes point collections from several known "historic Papago village sites," and concludes that small, generally unnotched points with concave bases typify these sites and the most recent material from Ventana Cave.

Based on this research and additional material discussed below, two unnotched point styles (Straight Base Triangular and U-shaped Base Triangular) may tentatively be assigned to the time after the end of the Classic period. Both of these styles lack notches, and in this analysis are primarily differentiated based on the degree of basal concavity. These two styles appear to be very common in surface contexts in the study area; 204 points in the collection were assigned to these two types.

Stemmed Small Points

Three different types of stemmed points are classified in the small point complex. Only 12 projectile points were assigned to these three-stemmed styles, which Sliva (1997) suggests are all associated with the Hohokam Colonial period. Some of the stemmed projectile point styles discussed in previous sections on large points have a wide range of variation in size and include some very small examples. This is particularly true of Late Archaic/Early Formative Cienega styles.

Justice grouped most stemmed small points into one style (Hodges Contracting Stem) in the Snaketown cluster. He defines Hodges Contracting Stem as "a triangular form with a short contracting stem and often strong serrations" (Justice 2002:287). The examples illustrated for this style exhibit considerable morphological variation, and all small points with contracting stems appear to be included. However, one example (Justice 2002:280 Figure 33.29) has a parallel-sided stem and others have only slightly contracting stems. Temporal estimates for this style appear to be largely consistent with the period of manufacture suggested by Sliva (1997). Justice argues these points are diagnostic of the Rillito phase (A.D. 700 to 900) at the Hodges site in Arizona. Justice suggests over 80 examples were collected from Snaketown, primarily from the Santa Cruz and Gila Butte phases of the Colonial period. He identifies further examples from the Stove Canyon phase (roughly A.D. 600 to 900) at Point of Pines (Justice 2002:287).

Stemmed Barbed

These projectile points have narrow triangular blades that are serrated with pairs of barbs at the base, slightly expanding stems, and convex bases (Figure 5h). This type appears to be uncommon in the study area, with only two examples in the collection. Sliva (1997:52) argues that these points are a Gila Butte phase style (roughly A.D. 750 to 850). Both of the Stemmed Barbed points in the collection are made from chert.

Table 22. Average Dimensions for Stemmed Barbed Points in the Collection

Attribute	Range	Average	Sample Size
Length	20.5 mm	20.5 mm	n=1
Neck Width	4.2 mm – 4.7mm	4.5 mm	n=2
Greatest Thickness	3.4 mm –4.3 mm	3.8 mm	n=2
Base Width	3.5 mm – 5.1 mm	4.3 mm	n=2
Blade Width	8.8 mm – 10.7 mm	9.8 mm	n=2

Stemmed Shouldered

Sliva (1997:52) suggests that this small point style dates to the Gila Butte phase (roughly A.D. 750 to 850). These points have long triangular blades, narrow slightly contracting stems, and abrupt shoulders (Figure 5i). Only three examples of this style (one of which is serrated) are present in the collection. Two of the points are chert, and the remaining example is rhyolite.

Table 23. Average Dimensions for Stemmed Shouldered Points in the Collection

Attribute	Range	Average	Sample Size
Length	19.1 mm – 30.5 mm	24.8 mm	n=2
Neck Width	3.4 mm – 6.8 mm	4.7 mm	n=3
Greatest Thickness	3.0 mm – 5.4 mm	4.0 mm	n=3
Base Width	2.8 mm – 5.4 mm	4.2 mm	n=3
Blade Width	11.8 mm – 16.1 mm	13.6 mm	n=3

Stemmed Tanged

This style is also thought to have been produced in the Hohokam Colonial period (approximately A.D. 750 to 950). These points have long triangular blades, narrow contracting stems, and barbed shoulders (Figure 5j). This style is also relatively uncommon in the study area, with only seven examples in the collection. Four of these points (57%) are serrated. Six (86%) are chert, and a single (14%) example is made from chalcedony.

Hoffman classified Stemmed Tanged and Stemmed Shouldered as a single style (Snaketown Stemmed), with chronological variants. He suggests that the style first appeared during the Pioneer period and continued into the Colonial period. In his typology, the Snaketown phase points lack serrations and have convex to straight blades; Gila Butte phase points are serrated with convex to straight blades; and Santa Cruz phase variants are serrated with concave blade margins and short stems. However, he notes that "the validity of this interpretation has not yet been demonstrated" (Hoffman 1997:183).

Table 24. Average Dimensions for Stemmed Tanged Points in the Collection

Attribute	Range	Average	Sample Size
Length	17.5 mm – 42.0 mm	28.1 mm	n= 5
Neck Width	3.4 mm – 5.3 mm	4.6 mm	n=7
Greatest Thickness	2.3 mm – 4.6 mm	3.5 mm	n=7
Base Width	2.9 mm – 15.0 mm	9.7 mm	n=5
Blade Width	9.2 mm – 15.0 mm	13.0 mm	n=7

Side-Notched Styles

Small side-notched points appear to have been produced in the Sedentary and Classic periods, but may have rarely been made after the Classic period in the study area. Small side-notched styles in the collection are largely triangular forms, and were differentiated based on notching width and position on the blade. These points were relatively common, with 122 examples in the collection considered here.

Side-notched points were separated into five styles. The first three styles have notches located near the lower third of the blade. This was by far the most common notch placement in the collection with a combined total of 101 projectile points. These three styles are then distinguished based on the width of the notches. Points with wide notches (14 examples) tend to be thick and those with narrow notches (10 examples) are generally thinner. Both the Narrow Side-Notched and Wide Side-Notched styles are generally larger than the Intermediate Side-Notched styles (77 examples). Upper Side-Notched (3 examples) style points have, as the name suggests, side notches in the upper third of the blade. Finally, Middle Side-Notched (18 examples) points have notches near the midpoint of the blade.

Hoffman (1997:206–210) grouped the narrow, wide, and intermediate side-notched points into a single style he labeled "Sauceda Side-notched." He excluded serrated points from this style, and the side-notched points considered here also almost always lack serration. Not surprisingly, he found that "Sauceda Side-notched" points were recovered from Pioneer through Classic period contexts, although most "were associated with the Sacaton phase" (Hoffman 1997:209). This patterning is largely consistent with the temporal assignment suggested by Sliva (1997).

Justice (2002:289–319) classified side-notched points in the Pueblo Side Notched and Chaco clusters. Although not systematically differentiated, he defines 10 styles for the Pueblo Side-Notched cluster. He does not consistently employ notch position on the blade or notch width to differentiate types, which complicates comparisons between his types and the Sliva types. Distribution maps presented by Justice suggest that 6 of the Pueblo Side-Notched cluster styles occur in the project area; however, examples that are similar to those illustrated for all 10 styles, including some of the more unusual types, are present in the collection considered here.

At least two examples of double side-notched points (Figures 6a and 6b) were collected. Justice (2002) includes double side-notched points in two types (White Mountain Side-Notched and Buck Taylor Notched), both of which also include single notched examples. Interestingly, limited data suggest the distinctive double notching pattern is in at least some instances associated with Apache or Yavapai occupations (Breternitz 1960; Justice 2002:312–315).

Though rare, side-notched points with a notch centrally located in the base occur in the middle Gila collection (Figures 6c and 6d). Justice classifies these points as Awatovi Side-Notched and suggests they appear starting around A.D. 1250 to 1300 and exist until the end of the nineteenth century (Justice 2002:317). As is the case for other side-notched styles,

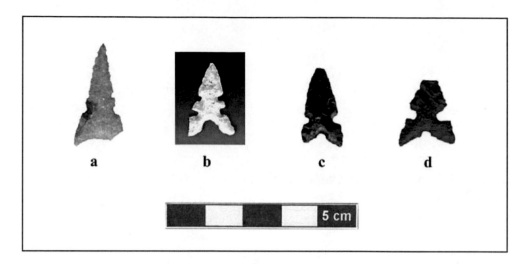

**Figure 6. Atypical Side-Notching Styles in the Middle Gila Point
Collection, Gila River Indian Community.**

this distinctive notching pattern occurs at Late Prehistoric sites throughout much of the western United States and is classified differently on a regional basis.

Because the importance of these artifacts is easily exaggerated, point styles that are rare or idiosyncratic in collections must be interpreted with caution. While it might be tempting to suggest Apache incursions or Pueblo migrations based on what appear to be distinctively different points, a number of other explanations may account for their presence and this single line of evidence is not sufficient to support any such argument.

Justice (2002:246–260) distinguishes three side-notched types (Bonito Notched, Pueblo Alto Side-Notched, and Pueblo Del Arroyo Notched) in the Chaco cluster. Not surprisingly, Justice suggests that none of the point types in this cluster occur in the middle Gila area. Convex blade margins and convex bases are common for Chaco cluster side-notched points, whereas this form of blade and base treatment is rare for side-notched points in the collection considered here. Further, some of the Chaco cluster points have a distinctive pattern of two side notches on one blade margin and a single notch on the opposite blade margin, and only one possible example of this notching pattern was identified in the collection considered here. However, some of the Chaco cluster points are stylistically indistinguishable from points in the middle Gila collection, particularly those in the Pueblo Alto Side-Notched type.

Narrow Side-Notched

These side-notched points have triangular blades that are thin with straight blade margins, and straight to concave bases (Figure 7a). The notches on this style are narrow and deep. Serration is also rare for this type, and only a single serrated point was classified as

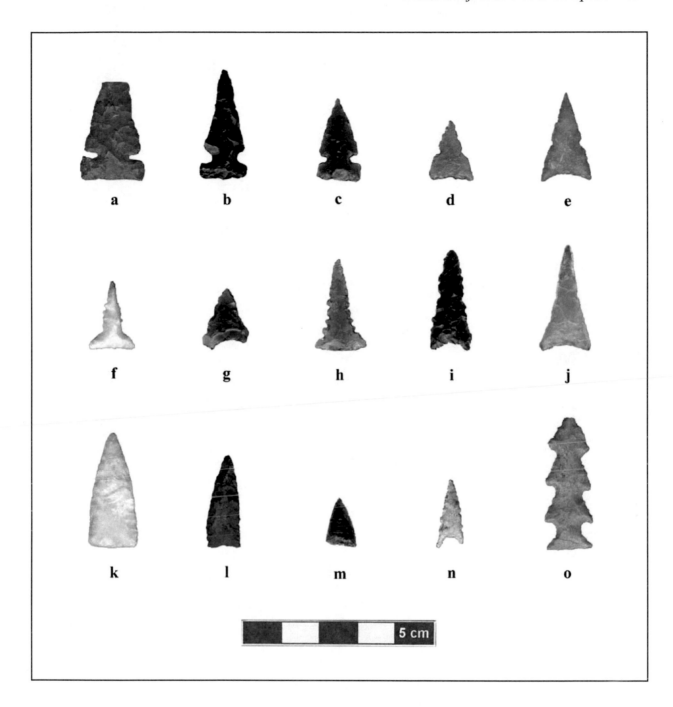

Figure 7. Hohokam Classic, Protohistoric/Historic, and Eccentric Projectile Points from the Gila River Indian Community: a) Narrow Side-Notched; b) Wide Side-Notched; c) Intermediate Side-Notched; d) Upper Side-Notched; e) Middle Side-Notched; f) Flanged; g) Bulbous Base; h) Concave Blade; i) Straight Blade Serrated; j) Concave Base Triangular; k) Thin Triangular; l) Long Triangular; m) Straight Base Triangular; n) U-shaped Base Triangular; o) Eccentric.

Table 25. Average Dimensions for Narrow Side-Notched Points in the Collection

Attribute	Range	Average	Sample Size
Length	36.3 mm – 42.8 mm	38.7 mm	n=3
Neck Width	36.3 mm – 42.8 mm	7.6 mm	n=10
Greatest Thickness	2.6 mm – 3.9 mm	3.2 mm	n=10
Base Width	12.5 mm – 19.4 mm	15.2 mm	n= 6
Blade Width	11.4 mm – 15.3 mm	13.8 mm	n=10

Narrow Side-Notched. These points are generally broken, probably because they are comparatively thin for their size. Sliva (1997:53) suggests that these points were made between A.D. 950 and 1150 in southern Arizona and between A.D. 900 and 1300 on the Colorado Plateau. Surprisingly, the 10 examples of this style in the collection are exclusively chert.

Wide Side-Notched

This style has "triangular blades, side notching on the point forming a short base, and straight to slightly concave bases" (Sliva 1997:53). As the name indicates, these points have wide side notches (Figure 7b). Sliva suggests that this point style is from the Sedentary period (roughly A.D. 950 to 1150) in southern Arizona. These points are somewhat common in the study area, with 14 examples of this style in the collection. None of the examples is serrated. Chert is the most common material, with 9 (64%) examples. Four (29%) Wide Side-Notched points are obsidian, and a single (7%) point is quartz. Sliva (1997:53) suggests that these points were made between A.D. 950 and 1150 in southern Arizona and between A.D. 900 and 1300 on the Colorado Plateau.

Justice (2002:310–311) appears to have defined this style as Snaketown Side-Notched; however, the Gatlin Side-Notched style is not clearly differentiated. "While most triangular side notched points have narrow notches, Snaketown Side Notched exhibits wide U-shaped notches placed low on the preform that are widest at the notch opening" (Justice 2002:311). Although according to Justice this type was the most commonly identified at Snaketown, he suggests it was made between A.D. 1200 to 1400 during the Classic period.

Table 26. Average Dimensions for Wide Side-Notched Points in the Collection

Attribute	Range	Average	Sample Size
Length	26.0 mm – 41.4 mm	31.0 mm	n=7
Neck Width	5.6 mm – 11.3 mm	7.4 mm	n=14
Greatest Thickness	3.2 mm – 5.4 mm	4.0 mm	n=14
Base Width	11.0 mm – 17.0 mm	13.9 mm	n=12
Blade Width	9.1 mm – 15.4 mm	11.7 mm	n=14

Intermediate Side-Notched

These small, triangular points have side notches in the lower one-third of the blade margin (Figure 7b) that are intermediate in width between the wide-notched and narrow-notched styles. These points are one of the most common styles in the collection, with 77 examples identified. The large number of projectile points assigned to this type is probably partially the result of the considerable time period over which similar side-notched points appear to have been used. If possible, subdivision of this style into two or more temporally relevant types will be an important research issue for future analyses.

These points are rarely serrated: only 6 (8%) examples exhibit this form of edge treatment. Prehistoric flint knappers showed a remarkably strong preference for obsidian with this style: 55 (71%) of these points are obsidian. Chert was the next most common material with 14 (18%) examples. Four (5%) of these points are chalcedony, 3 (4%) are rhyolite, and a single example (1%) is basalt.

Sliva separated Intermediate Side-Notched points into 2 styles; she suggests that one style (Sedentary Intermediate Notched) was made between A.D. 950 and 1150 in southern Arizona and between A.D. 900 and 1300 on the Colorado Plateau. Sliva (1997:54) argues that the second style (Late Classic Side-Notched) was made from A.D. 1300 through 1450 in southern Arizona and A.D. 1000 to 1450 on the Colorado Plateau.

It also possible that use of this style continued into the Protohistoric/Historic period within the study area. This possibility is suggested by a point of this style that was illustrated by Russell (1908:110) as an example of points that were collected from earlier sites and reused by the O'odham near the beginning of the twentieth century.

Table 27. Average Dimensions for Intermediate Side-Notched Points in the Collection

Attribute	Range	Average	Sample Size
Length	13.4 mm – 36.2 mm	21 mm	n=54
Neck Width	3.1 mm – 10.1 mm	4.7 mm	n=74
Greatest Thickness	1.8 mm – 5.2 mm	3 mm	n=75
Base Width	8.0 mm – 18.8 mm	17.9 mm	n=64
Blade Width	6.1 mm – 15.4 mm	9.5 mm	n=70

Upper Side-Notched

These points differ from other side-notched points in that the notches are above the midpoint of the blade edge (Figure 7d). This creates a long base (tang) and, consequently, hafting the point would require a deep split (or notch) in the arrow shaft. These points are rare in the study area, and only three examples were identified in the collection. Two of these points are made from chert, and the remaining example is obsidian. Sliva argues that these points were made during the earlier portion of the Classic period (roughly A.D. 1050 to 1150); however, it is not possible to test this suggestion for local examples using currently available data.

This distinctive style may be considerably more common in other areas. For example, this point type appears to be substantially more common at Salado sites in the Tonto Basin, especially the Bass Point Platform mound site where they were classified as Upper Side-Notched (Rice 1994:301). Upper Side-Notched points were largely made from obsidian (Rice 1994:305), and it is possible their manufacture was, in part, associated with the use of very small obsidian nodules.

Table 28. Average Dimensions for Early Classic Side-Notched Points in the Collection

Attribute	Range	Average	Sample Size
Length	15.5 mm – 18.2 mm	16.7 mm	n=3
Neck Width	5.6 mm – 7.0 mm	6.3 mm	n=3
Greatest Thickness	2.7 mm – 4.4 mm	3.3 mm	n=3
Base Width	10.6 mm – 13.1 mm	11.8 mm	n=3
Blade Width	4.1 mm – 6.1 mm	5.4 mm	n=3

Middle Side-Notched

These points have side notches near the middle of the point edges, forming a long base (Figure 7a). The point bases are straight to concave, blade margins are straight, and only one (6%) of the 18 examples of this style is serrated. The most common material for these points is chert: 14 (78%) examples are chert and the remaining 4 (22%) are obsidian.

Sliva argues that these points were produced largely during the middle portion of the Classic period; however, it is not possible to test this suggestion for the study area using currently available data. Sliva (1997:54) suggests that these points were made from A.D. 1050 through 1350 in southern Arizona and A.D. 1000 to 1450 on the Colorado Plateau.

Hoffman (1997:210–214) appears to have included the Upper and Middle Side-Notched points as a single type he labeled "Salado Side-notched." Although his sample included a limited number of points from dated contexts, nearly all of those that could be attributed to a phase were assigned to the Civano phase of the Classic period.

Justice (2002) includes four styles (Pueblo Side-Notched, Ridge Ruin Side-Notched, Point of Pines Side-Notched, and Walnut Canyon Side-Notched) that have examples of side notching near the midpoint of the blade. As previously noted, however, Justice did not use notch placement to distinguish types, and the Pueblo Side-Notched type in particular includes a substantial range of variation in morphological appearance. Interestingly, examples of Middle Side-Notched points made from bone and antler were recovered from Ridge Ruin, near Flagstaff Arizona (Justice 2002).

Table 29. Average Dimensions for Middle Side-Notched Points in the Collection

Attribute	Range	Average	Sample Size
Length	15.7 mm – 33.2 mm	22.6 mm	n=12
Neck Width	4.9 mm – 7.9 mm	6.2 mm	n=18
Greatest Thickness	1.8 mm – 3.8 mm	2.8 mm	n=18
Base Width	8.3 mm – 14.3 mm	11.3 mm	n=15
Blade Width	5.3 mm – 9.0 mm	7.0 mm	n=16

Unnotched Point Styles

Completed projectile points that lack notches or a stem are extremely common in the Gila River collection. As previously discussed, it is often difficult to distinguish late stage preforms from points that were completed but never notched, serrated, or stemmed. This factor has been a source of considerable variation in how previous researchers have classified points. Some have not attempted to separate preforms, while others appear to have assumed that all points lacking notches, serration, or a stem are unfinished. The first approach results in overestimation of the incidence of unnotched points, while the second underestimates the incidence.

All unnotched point styles in Hoffman's (1997) typology are serrated. He did include stemless points without serration in his initial taxonomic classification, but these points were excluded from the stylistic classification on which his analysis was based. It is unclear why these points were excluded, but he probably considered them to be preforms. Some of the examples he illustrates for the "Colinas Serrated" type do not appear to have distinct serrations. Determining whether blade edges were intentionally serrated or simply irregularly finished is often difficult. In this analysis, only projectile points with distinct saw-tooth like edges were classified as serrated.

Justice (2002) defines four types of unnotched points, all of which he assigns to the Western Triangular cluster. In addition, the Snaketown cluster includes several types with unnotched points illustrated as examples. This is particularly true of the Snaketown Triangular Straight Base and the Snaketown Triangular Concave Base types, which include almost exclusively serrated or barbed examples of unnotched points. As Justice notes (2002:261), it is difficult to separate unnotched points into types, in large part because by their very nature these points lack the attributes that are usually employed to distinguish types.

Flanged

This unusual style has long, generally parallel-sided blades and concave flanged bases that are wider than the blade (Figure 7c). These points are occasionally serrated: 5 (24%) of the 21 examples in the collection are serrated. Sliva (1997:54) believes these points were made between A.D. 1050 and 1150, and possibly also during the late Classic period. Obsidian is the most common material type (n=9, 43%), followed by chert (n=7, 33%), basalt (n=3, 14%), chalcedony (n=1, 5%), and quartzite (n=1, 5%).

Justice (2002) does not appear to include any similar projectile points in his typology. This is surprising given the distinctive and unusual characteristics of these points, and because he examined points from the Snaketown collection that includes examples of this style (Hoffman 1997:154). One possibility is that Justice considers these artifacts to be drills. In this analysis, drills were separated from projectile points based on the presence of opposed steep angle edge retouch and usewear.

Hoffman appears to have included points similar to this style in a category that he named "Solares Corner-notched." This category, however, is defined differently and includes points that differ from most Classic Flanged points. He argues that these points were primarily produced during the Sacaton phase (Hoffman 1997:207), and indeed the production of Flanged points may have actually begun prior to the start of the Classic period.

Table 30. Average Dimensions for Flanged Points in the Collection

Attribute	Range	Average	Sample Size
Length	16.3 mm – 34.1 mm	24.9 mm	n=13
Neck Width	5.1 mm – 11.3 mm	7.5 mm	n=21
Greatest Thickness	2.4 mm – 5.9 mm	3.7 mm	n=21
Base Width	10.0 mm – 16.2 mm	12.4 mm	n=21
Blade Width	4.8 mm – 10.4 mm	8.2 mm	n=21

Bulbous Base

These unusual points are rare in the collection: only three points were classified as this style. Two examples are obsidian, and the remaining point is chert. These points have narrow blades, flange stems, and irregular concave bases (Figure 7g). Sliva (1997:56) argues that these points were made from A.D. 1250 through 1350. Neither Justice (2002) nor Hoffman (1997) include similar points in their classification systems, suggesting these points generally are absent or only occur in low frequencies.

Table 31. Average Dimensions for Classic Bulbous Base Points in the Collection

Attribute	Range	Average	Sample Size
Length	14.9 mm – 19.8 mm	17.3 mm	n=2
Neck Width	6.7 mm – 6.9 mm	6.8 mm	n=3
Greatest Thickness	3.3 mm – 4.5 mm	4.0 mm	n=3
Base Width	10.9 mm – 12.4 mm	11.6 mm	n=2
Blade Width	5.4 mm – 6.9 mm	6.1 mm	n=3

Concave Blade

These points have serrated blade margins, straight to slightly concave bases, and moderately concave blade edges (Figure 7h). These points are comparatively common in the study area; 38 points were classified as this style. Sliva (1997:53) suggests that these points were made between A.D. 950 and 1150. Chert is the most common material type, with 17 (45%) examples in the collection. Obsidian is also common; 15 (39%) of the Concave Blade points are of this material. The remaining points are made from chalcedony (n=4, 11%) and quartz (n=2, 5%).

Hoffman referred to this style as Snaketown Serrated but does not appear to have differentiated it from other serrated styles. He observes, "Although examples of Snaketown Serrated points have been recovered from Snaketown through Sacaton/Soho contexts, the points in the sample are most commonly associated with the Sacaton phase" (Hoffman 1997:191).

Justice (2002) classified these points as Snaketown Triangular Concave Base or Snaketown Triangular Straight Base. Both of these styles, however, included barbed points that were classified as the Eccentric style in this analysis. Justice also includes more triangular forms with deeply concave bases in the Snaketown Triangular Concave Base, but in this analysis these points were classified as Straight Blade Serrated. Similar to Sliva (1997), Justice (2002:284–287) suggests both Snaketown Triangular Concave Base and Snaketown Triangular Straight Base are Sacaton phase styles.

Table 32. Average Dimensions for Concave Blade Points in the Collection

Attribute	Range	Average	Sample Size
Length	17.1 mm – 57.2 mm	26.5 mm	n=19
Neck Width	4.6 mm – 12.0 mm	7.2 mm	n=36
Greatest Thickness	2.2 mm – 4.6 mm	3.5 mm	n=37
Base Width	8.4 mm – 14.8 mm	10.8 mm	n=35
Blade Width	5.2 mm – 11.9 mm	8.3 mm	n=36

Straight Blade Serrated

Sliva (1997) refers to these points as Classic Serrated. These points lack notches, they have straight blade margins, and crescent to v-shaped shaped concave bases (Figure 7i). This style is similar to Large Concave Base Triangular except that the points are serrated, and they have narrower bases on average. Only nine examples of this style were identified in the collection. Sliva (1997:55) suggests that these points were made from A.D. 1050 through 1350 in southern Arizona and A.D. 1000 to 1450 on the Colorado Plateau. Obsidian is the most common material, with seven (78%) examples. Individual (11%) basalt and quartz points were classified as this style.

Hoffman appears to have classified this style as "Colinas Serrated." Almost 95 percent of these points in the collection that he analyzed were recovered from Classic period contexts, which is consistent with the temporal assignment suggested here. Justice (2002) includes points of this style in his Snaketown Triangular Concave Base and Cottonwood Triangular; however, both types include other dissimilar points.

Table 33. Average Dimensions for Straight Blade Serrated Points in the Collection

Attribute	Range	Average	Sample Size
Length	19.7 mm – 37.2 mm	24.5 mm	n=7
Neck Width	5.6 mm – 11.3 mm	8.5 mm	n=9
Greatest Thickness	2.5 mm – 5.8 mm	3.7 mm	n=9
Base Width	9.1 mm – 16.4 mm	11.6 mm	n=9
Blade Width	6.4 mm – 11.8 mm	8.5 mm	n=9

Concave Base Triangular

These projectile points lack notches or a stem; they have straight to slightly concave blade margins and deeply concave bases that are V-shaped rather than U-shaped (Figure 7j). These points also have wider bases on average than Large Thin Triangular points exhibit. Only 11 examples of this style are present in the collection, none of which is serrated (serrated examples of this style are a separate category in the typology). Sliva (1997:55) suggests that these points were made from A.D. 1150 through 1350 in central Arizona and A.D. 1000 to 1450 on the Colorado Plateau. This style, made from a surprising diversity of materials, is the only type for which chalcedony is most common. Four (36%) points are chalcedony, three (27%) are basalt, two (18%) are chert, and two (18%) are obsidian.

The Hoffman (1997) stylistic typology does not include points of this type. Justice (2002:261) classified these points as Cottonwood Triangular, a "catchall type that subsumes a large range of variation." Not surprisingly, he suggests these points have a long span of manufacture, beginning in A.D. 900 and continuing into the Historic period (Justice 2002:265).

Table 34. Average Dimensions for Concave Base Triangular Points in the Collection

Attribute	Range	Average	Sample Size
Length	17.4 mm – 27.6 mm	22.7 mm	n=7
Neck Width	5.2 mm – 11.2 mm	9.1 mm	n=10
Greatest Thickness	2.2 mm – 4.2 mm	3.2 mm	n=11
Base Width	9.9 mm – 15.5 mm	12.9 mm	n=10
Blade Width	5.0 mm – 10.6 mm	8.3 mm	n=9

Thin Triangular

These points have straight to slightly concave bases, they lack notching (Figure 7k), and they are differentiated from other unnotched styles "on the basis of their uniform thinness" (Sliva 1997:54). Five of the nine (56%) examples of this style are serrated. Chert is by far the most common material, with seven (78%) of the nine examples made from this material. Individual (11%) basalt and obsidian points were assigned to this style. Sliva (1997:54) argues that these points were made between A.D. 1050 and 1350. Neither Justice (2002) nor Hoffman (1997) defined a similar type.

Table 35. Average Dimensions for Thin Triangular Points in the Collection

Attribute	Range	Average	Sample Size
Length	14.7 mm – 30.1 mm	22.2 mm	n=7
Neck Width	6.6 mm – 13.8 mm	9.5 mm	n=8
Greatest Thickness	1.7 – 4.21 mm	2.4 mm	n=9
Base Width	8.6 mm – 14.2 mm	11.9 mm	n=8
Blade Width	5.7 mm – 13.1 mm	9.1 mm	n=7

Long Triangular

These unnotched points have straight to slightly concave bases, straight blade margins, and a length-to-width of roughly 3:1 (Figure 7l). These points are somewhat common in the study area: 13 examples were identified in the collection. Sliva (1997:55) suggests that this style was made from A.D. 1050 through 1450 in southern Arizona and A.D. 1000 to 1450 on the Colorado Plateau. Basalt and chert are equally common for this style, with 6 (46%) examples each, and the single remaining point (8%) is chalcedony. This style was also not differentiated by either Justice (2002) or Hoffman (1997).

Table 36. Average Dimensions for Long Triangular Points in the Collection

Attribute	Range	Average	Sample Size
Length	21.9 mm – 39.7 mm	26.3 mm	n=11
Neck Width	4.7 mm – 11.1 mm	8.7 mm	n=13
Greatest Thickness	2.0 mm – 4.5 mm	3.6 mm	n=13
Base Width	7.3 mm – 13.2 mm	10.6 mm	n=13
Blade Width	4.8 mm – 10.5 mm	8.5 mm	n=13

Straight Base Triangular

These small triangular points lack notches or a stem and have straight to slightly concave bases (Figure 7m). This style was differentiated from other unnotched styles on the basis of their roughly straight bases and length to width ratios of less than 1:3. These points were made from a wide diversity of materials. In contrast to most other small point styles, basalt is the most common material, accounting for 23 (36%) of the 64 points classified as Straight Base Triangular. Obsidian is the next most common, with 19 (30%) examples. Other materials present include chert (n=14, 22%), chalcedony (n=3, 5%), man-made glass (n=2, 3%), rhyolite (n=2, 3%), and quartzite (n=1, 2%). Serration is somewhat common for this style, with 22 (34%) serrated points of the 64 examples in the collection.

Sliva (1997:55) suggests that this style of point dates between A.D. 1050 and 1350. However, although these points could possibly have been made as early as A.D. 1050, site collections from Protohistoric/Historic period sites in the study area contain large numbers of them, including examples produced from man-made glass. In particular, the large collection of projectile points recovered from the Protohistoric/Historic Sacate site (GR-909) is dominated by small, unnotched, triangular forms with straight to slightly concave bases (Randolph et al. 2002).

Diagnostic artifacts suggest the Sacate village drifted along the Gila River bank from the location it initially occupied perhaps around A.D. 1750 until the 1950s. In contrast to other diagnostic types, projectile points from across the site show little variation in material types, or attribute data (Randolph et al. 2002:13–14) suggesting that a strong tradition in point manufacture existed over the roughly 200 years the site was occupied by the Akimel O'Odham. Straight Base Triangular points are highly similar to points Haury collected from historic Tohono O'odham village sites (Haury 1950). Brew and Huckell (1987) suggest that historical Akimel O'odham projectile points lack serrations, and are highly similar to those made by the Tohono O'odham. This suggestion is supported by the Sacate point assemblage, where less than 2% were serrated.

Table 37. Average Dimensions for Protohistoric/Historic Triangular Points in the Collection

Attribute	Range	Average	Sample Size
Length	10.2 mm – 24.6 mm	18.2 mm	n=58
Neck Width	5.4 mm – 12.7 mm	8.5 mm	n=63
Greatest Thickness	2.0 mm – 6.7 mm	3.1 mm	n=64
Base Width	7.6 mm – 14.0 mm	10.4 mm	n=62
Blade Width	3.8 mm – 10.9 mm	8.0 mm	n=60

U-shaped Base Triangular

These points are distinguished from other unnotched points based on their u-shaped concave bases, which form long tangs (Figure 7n). Separating Straight Base Triangular, U-shaped Base Triangular, and Concave Base Triangular types is often difficult because basal treatment has a continuous rather than modal distribution. U-shaped Base Triangular points are generally long and narrow, whereas Straight Base Triangular points are generally shorter and wider. Blade margins on U-shaped Base Triangular points are usually straight, whereas slightly convex blade margins are more common for other unnotched styles.

The U-shaped Base Triangular style is the most common identified, with 140 examples in the collection. The type, however, was not included in the Silva typology. Points assigned to this style generally lack serration, but 44 (31%) examples are serrated. Chert is the most commonly used material, with 56 (40%) examples. Of the remaining points, 46 (33%) are obsidian, 24 (17%) are basalt, 8 (6%) are chalcedony, 5 (4%) are man-made glass, and a single example (1%) is rhyolite.

Artifacts similar to the U-Shaped Base Triangular style were classified as "Sobaipuri" points by Justice (2002), a suggestion originally made based on Pfefferkorn's description of Sonoran points (Ravesloot and Whittlesey 1987:95). Most definitions of "Sobaipuri" points (Brew and Huckel 1987; Justice 2002:272), however, are different than that employed here, and they are usually restricted to serrated points with deeply concave bases that lack notches. While examples that fit this definition are present in the middle Gila collection, most of the unnotched points with deeply concave bases lack serration.

Table 38. Average Dimensions for O'odham Points in the Collection

Attribute	Range	Average	Sample Size
Length	9.2 mm – 27.5 mm	17.7 mm	n=116
Neck Width	3.8 mm – 11.2 mm	7.5 mm	n=135
Greatest Thickness	1.4 mm – 7.4 mm	3.2 mm	n=139
Base Width	7.0 mm – 16.2 mm	10.5 mm	n=129
Blade Width	3.7 mm – 10.8 mm	7.3 mm	n=137

60

Protohistoric/Historic Point Discussion

Ravesloot and Whittlesey (1987:96) argued that "small, triangular, concave-based points with serrated edges were being produced in the Classic Period." While this is certainly the case and, in fact, points fitting this description appear to occur as early as the Sedentary period, some data suggest that distinctive Protohistoric/Historic styles may still be identified. One of the primary goals for the ongoing projectile points analysis will be to recognize traits or combinations of traits that most consistently identify projectile points made after the Classic period.

Preliminary analysis of Protohistoric/Historic collections suggests that in particular, very deeply concave U-shaped bases are a comparatively recent phenomenon in the middle Gila region. However, some side-notched points in the collection have deeply concave U-shaped bases, and neither U-shaped bases nor serration alone can be exclusively employed to identify late points. At the same time, variation among points from contemporaneous Protohistoric/Historic sites suggests that the set of attributes used to define "Sobaipuri" style may indeed reflect a distinct type associated with late occupations.

Village site GR-1139 is located approximately 3.2 kilometers to the west of GR-909 on the south side of the Gila River along Santa Cruz wash. Numerous small points were collected from each site (GR-909, n=96; GR-1139, n=73) and both were occupied during the Late Historic Period. GR-1139, however, also has evidence for Pioneer to Classic period Hohokam occupation in some Loci (Eiselt et al. 2002), which is largely absent from GR-909 (Randolph et al. 2002).

Figure 8 shows selected examples of projectile points collected from GR-1139 and GR-909. These points were selected to represent the range of variation in basal and edge treatment for unnotched points at the two sites. Projectile points that fit the common definition of "Sobaipuri" points (Brew and Huckell 1987; Doelle 1984; Justice 2002:272) occur at GR-1139, but only two poor examples of this type were found at GR-909. The relatively close proximity and roughly contemporaneous occupation of these two sites during the Historic period suggest that the lack of "Sobaipuri" style points at GR-909 is not simply the product of spatial or temporal variation.

In general, highly similar small points were recovered from these sites, including points produced from man-made glass. However, the incidence of serration, U-shaped Base Triangular, and Straight Base Triangular points differs dramatically between them. Only slightly over 2% of the completed small points from GR-909 were serrated, whereas 30% of the completed small points from GR-1139 had this form of edge treatment. Although it is difficult to completely rule out temporal variation, Loci at GR-1139 that have predominantly historical artifacts also have high incidences of serration. For example, "[h]istorical-period materials dominate the artifact assemblage" (Eiselt et al. 2002:474) from Locus M at GR-1139, and 35% of the 26 points from this locus were serrated.

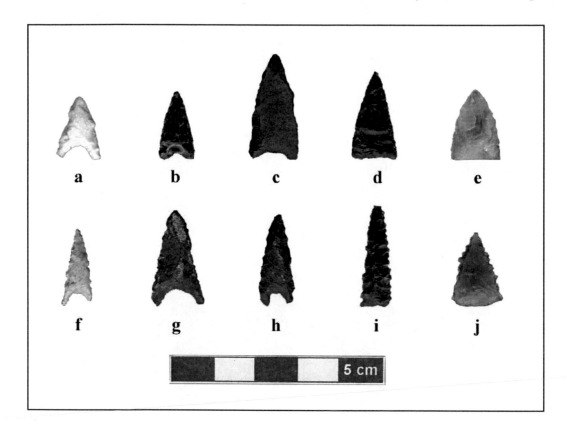

Figure 8. Selected Examples of Projectile Points from GR-909 (a-e) and GR-1139 (f-j), Gila River Indian Community.

U-shaped Base Triangular points outnumber Straight Base Triangular points over 4 to 1 at GR-1139, whereas U-shaped Base Triangular points are only slightly more common than Straight Base Triangular points at GR-909. Although not systematically measured during the analysis, deeply concave bases appear to be substantially more common at GR-1139.

Material type frequencies also differ substantially between the two sites. Basalt was used for 47% of the small points at GR-909, whereas this material comprised just 4% of the collection from GR-1139. Obsidian and chert were far more common at GR-1139 (88% of the collection), than at GR-909 (42% of the collection). Because point attributes vary with material type, it could be argued that the apparent stylistic variation between GR-909 and GR-1139 is the product of raw material constraints. This suggestion is based on the possibility that the generally higher fracture toughness of some materials like basalt made them extremely difficult to serrate. This possibility is supported by the observation that only 6% of the small basalt points in the entire collection are serrated. In contrast, materials with lower fracture toughness were much more likely to be serrated; 31% of the small chert points and 24% of the small obsidian points are serrated.

Raw material constraints, however, cannot fully account for the substantial variation between points from GR-909 and GR-1139. Points made from low-fracture toughness materials that could have been serrated comprise almost half the collection from GR-909, but this form of treatment is extremely rare for all material types at the site. In addition, none of the materials used to make points at GR-909 were available at the site itself, and if serration or other aspects that are difficult to execute with basalt were considered important, it is unlikely this material would have been imported in large quantities.

The middle Gila data support the suggestion by Ravesloot and Whittlesey (1987:272–273) that the designation of unnotched points with serration and concave bases as "Sobaipuri" is unwarranted. Attribute data for Straight Base Triangular points (that is, "Pima or Papago" points) and U-shaped Base Triangular (that is, "Sobaipuri" points) fall along a continuum, and the two styles merely represent extremes of that range. Data of this nature cannot be used alone to suggest the existence of separate and distinct cultural traditions. The differences observed in the point assemblages from GR-909 and GR-1139 are almost certainly explained by factors in addition to being inhabited by "Pima" and "Sobaipuri" peoples respectively.

Eccentric

This category, added to the Sliva typology for this study, includes only eight unusual points, most of which (75%) are deeply serrated or barbed (Figure 7o). Individual points in this category are largely idiosyncratic, and all unusually elaborate points in the collection were assigned to this style. Chert is the most common material, with six (75%) examples. Individual examples (12%) of basalt and chalcedony were also collected.

Temporal placement of this style is somewhat problematic. Hoffman (1997) divided these points into two main styles he termed Snaketown Barbed and Santan Barbed. As the name suggests, the majority (86%) of Snaketown Barbed points were recovered from cremations at Snaketown. These points were collected from Pioneer, Colonial, and Sedentary contexts (Hoffman 1997:225). However, they were most commonly associated with Gila Butte and Santa Cruz contexts (A.D. 750 to 950). Santan Barbed points were also largely (88%) recovered from Snaketown cremations in the sample examined by Hoffman (1997:229). These points were collected from both Colonial and Sedentary contexts but were most frequently from Sacaton phase (A.D. 950 to 1150) contexts (Hoffman 1997:230).

These points were relatively common at Snaketown but were largely recovered from cremations and were not common in other contexts at the site (Haury 1976). Consequently, it is not surprising that this style is rare in the collection considered here, because artifacts were rarely collected from burial areas. Other typologies (for example, Crabtree 1973; Hoffman 1997) have separated this style into two or more categories; however, because of the rarity of these points, all were included in a single category for the present study. Crabtree (1973) argues that these elaborate points were produced by a few specialized craftsmen and "were intended to fulfill needs other than day-to-day hunting and self-protection" (Crabtree quoted in Haury 1976:296). This suggestion is based largely on the assumption that the points are too large and elaborate to have been used, and the fact that they were generally recovered from cremation contexts (Haury 1976:296).

While these points indeed may not have been intended for mundane tasks, some could have been employed in a specialized activity such as fishing. In a recent review of over 100 ethnographic examples of stone point use, one of the only three cases where stone points were not used for hunting or warfare involved the use of stone projectile tips for fishing (Ellis 1997). The use of arrows for "hunting fishes" was documented among the Akimel O'odham by Captain Frederick E. Grossmann, an Indian agent in 1870–1871 (Kroeber and Fontana 1986:76). In addition, modern fishing arrows are considerably heavier than hunting arrows (to facilitate penetration of the water) and have barbs to retain the fish.

Table 39. Average Dimensions for Eccentric Points in the Collection

Attribute	Range	Average	Sample Size
Length	25.9 mm – 35.8 mm	29.7 mm	n=4
Neck Width	5.2 mm – 8.9 mm	6.7 mm	n=7
Greatest Thickness	2.3 mm – 7.0 mm	4.0 mm	n=8
Base Width	5.9 mm – 16.2 mm	10.9 mm	n=7
Blade Width	8.8 mm – 12.8 mm	11.1 mm	n=8

CHAPTER 4

SUMMARY

This document provides a preliminary discussion of variability in the projectile points collected as of the summer of 2002 from the Gila River Indian Community. Projectile points and point preforms are by far the most common type of retouched tool recovered from the project area. The points in the collection exhibit considerable variation in form and size. At least 268 examples appear to be Archaic styles. Archaic points, however, were frequently collected from sites that have evidence of occupation later in the Prehistoric period. Some of the points may have been collected and used by the inhabitants of later sites, but others likely derive from earlier occupations of the sites where they were found. This issue of reuse versus earlier components at sites is currently being evaluated through an examination of the spatial distribution of different point styles and other indications such as usewear and reworking.

In general, the incidence of projectile points appears to have increased steadily through time. This apparent diachronic increase in projectile points could result from several factors. First, the most simplistic explanation is that a steady increase occurred over time in the number of people who were occupying the study area. Second, older projectile points are more likely to be rare simply because they have experienced a greater period of time in which they could be buried by deposition, reworked, or otherwise removed from the archaeological record. Third, sites with structural remains and substantial midden deposits are more likely to be recorded during surveys; these sites generally postdate the Archaic period, and this factor may have biased the sample toward later period sites. Fourth, the incidence of the activities that projectile points were used for (such as hunting or warfare) could have increased though time, resulting in greater projectile point manufacture per capita.

Raw material use appears to have varied through time, and to a lesser extent between different point styles manufactured roughly at the same time. Aspects of the temporal variation identified in the collection are consistent with patterning observed elsewhere, which supports the temporal validity of the classification scheme employed here at least at a general level.

Basalt was most common during the Middle Archaic period but decreased in popularity until the pre-Classic period, when the use of it may have largely stopped. Subsequently, the use of basalt appears to have once again increased, and it accounts for nearly one-fourth of the most recent points in the sample. Obsidian use appears to have peaked during the Classic period, a pattern identified elsewhere as well. Rhyolite appears to have been favored for San Pedro points, and at least some of these points may have been brought to the study area as finished products. Chert was commonly used throughout the sequence. Most other material types occur only in low frequencies.

Projectile points lacking notches are very common in the collection. Classification of these points is often problematical, in part because of the difficulty inherent in distinguishing them from discarded point preforms. This problem, however, is not considered to be a significant factor in this analysis, because preforms constitute roughly equal portions of the small and large point collections, whereas unnotched points are dramatically more common in the small point collection. If unnotched points were commonly misclassified as preforms, than the small point collection should have had a higher incidence of preforms.

Some researchers have even implied that all points lacking notches, a stem, or serrations are unfinished (Frison 1971; Hoffman 1997). Other explanations to account for unnotched points include temporal variation (Jelks 1993), attribution to different cultural groups (Warren 1984), and variation in performance characteristics (Christenson 1997). The common co-occurrence of notched and unnotched points in large numbers from comparatively well-dated contexts within individual Hohokam sites suggests that cultural and temporal variation are not primary explanations. As Christenson (1997:134) has argued, "Such wide-spread and basic differences are primarily functional and . . . spatial and temporal trends in point form are primarily generated by technological and ecological trends." Another possibility is that unnotched points were designed for use in conflict between humans, whereas most notched points were intended for large game hunting (Ahler 1992:46). This possibility will be addressed more fully in future research.

Points with serrated edges are also relatively common in the study area (30% of the collection), but the significance of this practice is unclear. Many Hohokam typologies have employed this characteristic to define categories in the system (for example, Hoffman 1997); however, the lack of strong temporal patterning in the incidence of serration treatment suggests that serration is a poor indicator of diachronic variation. Furthermore, variation in performance characteristics due to serration is unclear, although at least one observer of the O'odham during the early Historic period (Pfefferkorn 1989) suggests that serration made the points more dangerous.

The large size and considerable time depth of the GRIC-CRMP projectile point collection allows unprecedented examination of spatial and temporal patterning among projectile points from the Hohokam core area. This document offers a preliminary typology for the classification of projectile points from the middle Gila. This scheme, which is largely focused upon classifying temporal variation, will be employed to structure future analyses of points from the study area. The ongoing investigations, particularly the recovery of points from well-dated contexts in the study area, will allow further refinement of the types.

REFERENCES CITED

Ahler, S. A.
  1992   Use-Phase Classification and Manufacturing Technology in Plains Village Arrowpoints. In *Piecing Together the Past: Applications of Refitting Studies in Archaeology*, edited by J. L. Hofman and J. G. Enloe, pp. 36–62. BAR International Series 578. Archaeopress, Oxford, England.

  1983   Heat Treatment of Knife River Flint. *Lithic Technology* 12(1):1–8.

Ambler, J. R.
  1996   Dust Devil Cave and Archaic Complexes of the Glen Canyon Area. In *Glen Canyon Revisited*, edited by P. R. Geib, pp. 40–52. University of Utah Anthropological Papers No. 119. University of Utah Press, Salt Lake City.

Amsden, C. A.
  1935   The Pinto Basin Artifacts. In *The Pinto Basin Site: An Ancient Aboriginal Camping Ground in the California Desert*, edited by E. W. Campbell and W. H. Campbell, pp. 33–51. Southwest Museum Papers No. 9. Los Angeles.

Anderson, K.
  1992   Lithic Raw Material Sources in Arizona. In *Making and Using Stone Artifacts: Lithic Sites in Arizona*. SWCA, Tucson.

Andrefsky, W., Jr.
  1994   Raw-Material Availability and Technology. *American Antiquity* 59:21–34.

Bayham, F. E., D. H. Morris, and M. S. Shackley (editors)
  1986   *Prehistoric Hunter-Gatherers of South Central Arizona: The Picacho Reservoir Archaic Project*. Anthropological Field Studies No. 13. Office of Cultural Resource Management, Department of Anthropology, Arizona State University, Tempe.

Bayman, J. M., and M. S. Shackley
  1999   Dynamic of Hohokam Obsidian Circulation in the North American Southwest. *Antiquity* 73:836–845.

Bernard-Shaw, M.
  1988   Chipped Stone Artifacts. In *The 1982-1984 Excavations at Las Colinas: Material Culture*. Arizona State Museum Archaeological Series 162, vol. 4. Cultural Resource Management Division, Arizona State Museum, University of Arizona, Tucson, AZ.

Binford, L. R.
 1979   Organization and Formation Processes: Looking at Curated Technologies. *Journal of Anthropological Research* 35:255–272.

Bonnichsen, B. R., and J. D. Keyser
 1982   Three Small Points: A Cody Complex Problem. *Plains Anthropologist* 27(96): 137–144.

Breternitz, C. D.
 1960   Orme Ranch Cave, NA 6656. *Plateau* 33(2):25–39.

Brew, S. A., and B. B. Huckell
 1987   A Protohistoric Piman Burial and a Consideration of Piman Burial Practices. *Kiva* 52(3):163–191.

Bryan, K., and J. H. Toulouse
 1943   The San Jose Non-Ceramic Culture and Its Relation to a Puebloan Culture in New Mexico. *American Antiquity* 8(3):269–280.

Campbell, E. W., and W. H. Campbell (editors)
 1935   *The Pinto Basin Site: An Ancient Aboriginal Camping Ground in the California Desert.* Southwest Museum Papers No. 9. Los Angeles.

Christenson, A. L.
 1997   Side-Notched and Unnotched Arrowpoints: Assessing Functional Differences. In *Projectile Technology*, edited by H. Knecht, pp. 131–142. Plenum Press, New York.

Churchill, S. E.
 1993   Weapon Technology, Prey Size Selection, and Hunting Methods in Modern Hunter-Gatherers: Implications for Hunting in the Paleolithic and Mesolithic. In *Hunting and Animal Exploitation in the Later Paleolithic and Mesolithic of Eurasia*, edited by G. Peterkin, H. Bricker, and P. Mellars, pp. 11–24. Archaeological Papers of the American Anthropological Association No. 4.

Cotterell, B., and J. Kamminga
 1987   The Formation of Flakes. *American Antiquity* 52(4):675–708.

Crabtree, D. E.
 1973   Experiments in Replications: Hohokam Points. *Tebiwa* 16(1):10–45.

Del Bene, T. A., and D. Ford
 1982   *Archaeological Excavations in Blocks VI and VII, Navajo Indian Irrigation Project, San Juan County, New Mexico.* Navajo Nation Papers in Anthropology No. 13. Navajo Tribal Cultural Resource Management Program, Window Rock, Arizona.

Douglas, C. L., D. L. Jenkins and C. N. Warren
  1988   Spatial and Temporal Variability in Faunal Remains from Four Lake Mojave-Pinto Period Sites in the Mojave Desert. In *Early Human Occupation in Far Western North America: the Clovis-Archaic Interface,* edited by J. A. Willig, C. M. Aikens, and J. L. Fagan, pp. 131–144. Anthropological Papers No. 21. Nevada State Museum, Carson City.

Eiselt, B. S., M. K. Woodson, J. Touchin, and E. Davis
  2002   *A Cultural Resources Assessment of the Casa Blanca Management Area, Pima Maricopa Irrigation Project (P-MIP), Gila River Indian Community, Arizona, Part 1.* Pima-Maricopa Irrigation Project Report No. 8. Cultural Resource Management Program, Gila River Indian Community, Sacaton, AZ.

Ellis, C. J.
  1997   Factors Influencing the Use of Stone Projectile Tips: An Ethnographic Perspective. In *Projectile Technology*, edited by H. Knecht, pp. 37–74. Plenum Press, New York.

Flenniken, J. J., and A. W. Raymond
  1985   Morphological Projectile Point Typology: Replication Experimentation and Technological Analysis. *American Antiquity* 51:603–614.

Formby, D. E.
  1986   Pinto-Gypsum Complex Projectile Points from Arizona and New Mexico. *Kiva* 51(2):99–127.

Fowler, D. D., D. B. Madsen, and E. M. Hattori
  1973   *Prehistory of Southeastern Nevada.* Desert Research Institute Publications in Social Sciences No. 6. Reno.

Fredrickson, David A., and Joel W. Grossman
  1977   A San Dieguito Component at Buena Vista Lake, California. *The Journal of California Anthropology* 4(2):173–190.

Frison, G.
  1971   Shoshonean Antelope Procurement in the Upper Green River Basin, Wyoming. *Plains Anthropologist* 16:258–284.

Gilpin, D., and D. A. Phillips, Jr.
  1998   *The Prehistoric to Historic Transition Period in Arizona, Circa A.D. 1519 to 1692: A Component of the Arizona Historic Preservation Plan.* State Historic Preservation Office, Arizona State Parks, Phoenix.

Gladwin, H. S., E. W. Haury, E. B. Sayles, and N. Gladwin
  1937   *Excavations at Snaketown: Material Culture.* Medallion Paper No. 25, Gila Pueblo, Globe, Arizona [Reprinted 1965, University of Arizona Press, Tucson.]

Gregory, D. A. (editor)

1999   *Excavations in the Santa Cruz River Floodplain: The Middle Archaic Component at Los Pozos.* Anthropological Papers No. 20. Center for Desert Archaeology, Tucson.

Halbirt, C. D., and T. K. Henderson (editors)

1993   *Archaic Occupation on the Santa Cruz Flats: The Tator Hills Archaeological Project.* Northland Research, Tempe.

Harrington, M. R.

1933   *Gypsum Cave, Nevada.* Southwest Museum Papers No. 8. Los Angeles.

1957   *A Pinto Site at Little Lake, California.* Southwest Museum Papers No. 17. Los Angeles.

Haury, E. W.

1950   *The Stratigraphy and Archaeology of Ventana Cave.* University of Arizona Press, Tucson.

1976   *The Hohokam: Desert Farmers and Craftsmen—Excavations at Snaketown, 1964–1965.* University of Arizona Press, Tucson.

Hendricks, D.M.

1985   *Arizona Soils.* College of Agriculture, University of Arizona, Tucson.

Hoffman, C. M.

1988   Lithic Technology and Lithic Tool Production at Casa Buena. In *Excavations at Casa Buena: Changing Hohokam Land Use along the Squaw Peak Parkway*, Vol. 1, edited by J. B. Howard. Soil Systems Publications in Archaeology No. 11. Phoenix.

1997   *Alliance Formation and Social Interaction during the Sedentary Period: A Stylistic Analysis of Hohokam Arrowpoints.* Unpublished Ph.D. dissertation, Department of Anthropology, Arizona State University, Tempe.

Hoffman, T. L., and D. E. Doyel

1985   Ground Stone Tool Production in the New River Basin. In *Hohokam Settlement and Economic Systems in the Central New River Drainage, Arizona*, Vol. 2, edited by D. E. Doyel and M. D. Elson, pp. 521–564. Publications in Archaeology No. 4. Soil Systems, Phoenix.

Holmer, R. N.

1980a Projectile Points. In *Sudden Shelter*, edited by J. D. Jennings, A. R. Schroedl, and R. N. Holmer, pp. 63–84. University of Utah Anthropological Papers No. 103. University of Utah Press, Salt Lake City.

1980b Chipped Stone Projectile Points. In *Cowboy Cave*, edited by J. D. Jennings, pp. 31–38. University of Utah Anthropological Papers No. 104. University of Utah Press, Salt Lake City.

1986 Common Projectile Points of the Intermountain West. In *Anthropology of the Desert West; Essays in Honor of Jesse D. Jennings,* edited by Carol J. Condie and Don D. Fowler, pp. 89–115. Anthropologica Papers No. 110, University of Utah, Salt Lake City.

Huckell, B. B. (editor)
1984 *The Archaic Occupation of the Rosemont Area, Northern Santa Rita Mountains, Southeastern Arizona.* Archaeological Papers No. 147, Vol. 1. Cultural Resource Management Division, Arizona State Museum, University of Arizona, Tucson.

Huckell, B. B.
1988 Late Archaic Archaeology of the Tucson Basin: A Status Report. In *Recent Research of Tucson Basin Prehistory: Proceedings of the Second Tucson Basin Conference,* edited by W. H. Doelle and P. R. Fish, pp. 57–80. Anthropological Papers No. 10. Institute for American Research, Tucson.

1995 *Of Marshes and Maize: Preceramic Agriculture Settlements in the Cienega Valley, Southeastern Arizona.* Anthropological Papers of the University of Arizona No. 59. University of Arizona Press, Tucson.

1996a Middle to Late Holocene Stream Behavior and the Transition to Agriculture in Southeastern Arizona. In *Early Formative Adaptations in the Southern Southwest,* edited by B. J. Roth, pp. 27–36. Monographs in World Archaeology No. 25. Prehistory Press, Madison, Wisconsin.

1996b The Archaic Prehistory of the North American Southwest. *Journal of World Prehistory* 10(3):305–373.

Irwin-Williams, C.
1967 Picosa: The Elementary Southwestern Culture. *American Antiquity* 32:441–457.

1973 *The Oshara Tradition: Origins of Anasazi Culture.* Eastern New Mexico University Contributions in Anthropology 5(1). Paleo Indian Institute, Eastern New Mexico University, Portales.

Jelks, E. B.
1993 Observations on the Distribution of Certain Arrow-Point Types in Texas and Adjoining Regions. *Lithic Technology* 18:9–15.

Jenkins, D. L.
1987 Dating the Pinto Occupation at Rogers Ridge: A Fossil Spring Site in the Mojave Desert, California. *Journal of California and Great Basin Anthropology,* 9(2):214–231.

Jenkins, D. L., and C. N. Warren
  1984   Obsidian Hydration and the Pinto Chronology in the Mojave Desert. *Journal of California and Great Basin Anthropology* 6(1):44–60.

Jennings, J. D.
  1980   *Cowboy Cave.* University of Utah Anthropological Papers No. 104. University of Utah Press, Salt Lake City.

Jennings, J. D., A. R. Schroedl, and R. N. Holmer
  1980   *Sudden Shelter.* University of Utah Anthropological Papers No. 103. University of Utah Press, Salt Lake City.

Justice, N. D.
  2002   *Stone Age Spear and Arrow Points of the Southwestern United States.* Indiana University Press, Bloomington.

Kroeber, C. B., and B. Fontana
  1986   *Massacre on the Gila - An Account of the Last Major Battle Between American Indians, with Reflections on the Origin of War.* The University of Arizona Press, Tucson, AZ.

Loendorf, C. R.
  1997   Burial Practices at Cline Mesa Sites. In *Salado Residential Settlements on Tonto Creek,* by T. J. Oliver and D. Jacobs. Roosevelt Monograph Series 9, Anthropological Field Studies 38. Office of Cultural Resource Management, Department of Anthropology, Arizona State University, Tempe.

Lorentzen, Leon H.
  1998   Common Paleoindian and Archaic Projectile Points of Arizona. In *Paleoindian and Archaic Sites in Arizona,* edited by Jonathan B. Mabry, pp. 137–151. Technical Report No. 97-7, Center for Desert Archaeology, Tucson.

Mabry, J. B. (editor)
  1998   *Archaeological Investigations of Early Village Sites in the Middle Santa Cruz Valley: Analysis and Synthesis,* Part 2. Anthropological Papers No. 19. Center for Desert Archaeology, Tucson.

Mabry, J. B., D. L. Swartz, H. Wocherl, J. J. Clark, G. H. Archer, and M. W. Lindman
  1997   *Archaeological Investigations of Early Village Sites in the Middle Santa Cruz Valley, Descriptions of the Santa Cruz Bend, Square Hearth, Stone Pipe and Canal Sites.* Anthropological Papers No. 18. Center for Desert Archaeology, Tucson.

Mabry, J. B., M. K. Fraught, A. K. L. Freeman, and L. H. Lorentzen
  1998   *Paleoindian and Archaic Sites in Arizona.* Technical Report No. 97–7. Center for Desert Archaeology, Tucson.

Matson, R.G.
1991 *The Origins of Southwestern Agriculture*. The University of Arizona Press, Tucson.

McGregor, J. C.
1943 Burial of an Early American Magician. *Proceedings of the American Philosophical Society* 86(2):270–298.

Montero, L. G.
1993 Chipped Stone. In *Classic Period Occupation on the Santa Cruz Flats: The Santa Cruz Archaeological Project,* Part 2, edited by K. T. Henderson and R. J. Martynec, pp. 313–362. Northland Research, Flagstaff.

Ore, H. Thomas, and Claude N. Warren
1971 Late Pleistocene-Early Holocene Geomorphic History of Lake Mojave, California. Geological Society of

Parry, W. R., and R. L. Kelley
1997 Expedient Core Technology and Sedentism. In *The Organization of Core Technology*, edited by J. K. Johnson and C. A. Morrow, pp. 285–304. Westview Press, Boulder, Colorado.

Peterson, J. D.
1994 Chipped Stone. In *The Pueblo Grande Project, Vol. 4: Material Culture*. Soil Systems, Phoenix.

Pierce, H. W.
1985 Introduction–Geologic Framework of Arizona. In *Arizona Soils*, edited by D. M. Hendricks, pp. 12–32. College of Agriculture, University of Arizona, Tucson.

Pfefferkorn, I.
1989 *Sonora: A Description of the Province*, translated and annotated by T. E. Treutlein. University of Arizona Press, Tucson.

Randolph, B. G., J. A. Darling, C. Loendorf, and B. Rockette
2002 Historic Piman Structure and the Evolution of the Sacate Site (GR-909), Gila River Indian Community. In *Visible Archaeology on the Gila River Indian Reservation*, P-MIP Report No. 21. Cultural Resource Management Program, Gila River Indian Community, Sacaton, Arizona.

Ravesloot, J. C., and M. R. Waters
2004 Geoarchaeology and Archaeological Site Patterning on the Middle Gila River, Arizona. *Journal of Field Archaeology* 29(1, 2):203-214.

Ravesloot, J. C., and S. M. Whittlesey

1987   *The Archaeology of the San Xavier Bridge Site (AZ BB:13:14) Tucson Basin, Southern Arizona, Part 3.* Arizona State Museum Archaeological Series No. 171. Cultural Resource Management Division, Arizona State Museum, University of Arizona, Tucson.

Reynolds, S. J.

1985   *Geology of the South Mountains, Central Arizona.* Bulletin No. 195. Arizona Bureau of Geology and Mineral Technology, Geological Survey Branch.

Rice, G. E.

1994   Flaked- and Carved-Stone Collections of the Rock Island Complex. In *Where the Rivers Converge: Roosevelt Platform Mound Study, Report on the Rock Island Complex,* edited by O. Lindauer, pp. 291–316. Roosevelt Monograph Series No. 4, Anthropological Field Studies No. 33. Office of Cultural Resource Management, Department of Anthropology, Arizona State University, Tempe.

Rice, G. E., A. Simon, and C. Loendorf

1998   Production and Exchange of Economic Goods. In *A Synthesis of Tonto Basin Prehistory: the Roosevelt Archaeology Studies, 1989 to 1998,* edited by G. E. Rice, pp. 105–130. Anthropological Field Studies No. 41, Office of Cultural Resource Management, Department of Anthropology, Arizona State University, Tempe.

Rogers, M. J.

1939   *Early Lithic Industries of the Lower Basin of the Colorado River and Adjacent Desert Areas.* San Diego Museum of Man Papers No. 3.

Rosenthal, J. E., D. Brown, M. Severson, and J. B. Clonts

1978   *The Quijotoa Valley Project.* USDI National Park Service, Tucson.

Roth, B. J., and B. B. Huckell

1992   Cortaro Points and the Archaic of Southern Arizona. *Kiva* 57(4):353–370.

Rozen, K. C.

1984   Flaked Stone. In *Hohokam Habitation Sites in the Northern Santa Rita Mountains,* Vol. 1, Part 1. Arizona State Museum Archaeological Series No. 147. Cultural Resource Management Division, Arizona State Museum, University of Arizona, Tucson.

Russell, Frank

1908   *The Pima Indians.*   Twenty-sixth Annual Report of the Bureau of American Ethnology, 1904–1905, U.S. Government Printing Office, Washington, D.C.

Sayles, E. B., and E. V. Antevs

1941   *The Cochise Culture.* Medallion Papers 29. Gila Pueblo, Globe, Arizona.

Shackley, M. S.
  1988   Sources of Archaeological Obsidian in the Southwest: An Archaeological, Petrological, and Geochemical Study. *American Antiquity* 53:752–772.

Shott, M. J.
  1996   Innovation and Selection in Prehistory: A Case Study from the American Bottom. In *Stone Tools: Theoretical Insights into Human Prehistory,* edited by G. H. Odell, pp. 279–309. Plenum Press, New York.

Slaughter, M., L. A. K Fratt, and R. V. Ahlstrom
  1992   *Making and Using Stone Artifacts: A Context for Evaluating Lithic Sites in Arizona.* SWCA, Tucson.

Sliva, R. J.
  1997   *An Introduction to the Study and Analysis of Flaked Stone Artifacts and Lithic Technology.* Center for Desert Archaeology, Tucson.

  1999a Flaked Stone Artifacts. In *Excavations in the Santa Cruz River Floodplain: The Middle Archaic Component at Los Pozos,* edited by D. A. Gregory, pp. 33–45. Anthropological Papers No. 20. Center for Desert Archaeology, Tucson.

  1999b Cienega Points and Late Archaic Period Chronology in the Southern Southwest. *Kiva* 64(3):339–367.

  2001   Flaked Stone Artifacts. In *Excavations in the Santa Cruz River Floodplain: The Early Agricultural Component at Los Pozos,* edited by D. A. Gregory, pp. 91–106. Anthropological Papers No. 21. Center for Desert Archaeology, Tucson.

Thomas, D. H.
  1978   Arrowheads and Atlatl Darts: How the Stones Got the Shaft. *American Antiquity* 43:461–472.

  1981   How to Classify the Projectile Points from Monitor Valley, Nevada. *Journal of California and Great Basin Anthropology* 3(1):7–43.

Vaughn, S. J., and C. N. Warren
  1987   Toward a Definition of Pinto Points. *Journal of California and Great Basin Anthropology* 9(2):199–213.

Warren, C. N.
  1967   The San Dieguito Complex: A Review and Hypothesis. *American Antiquity* 32(2):168–185.

  1980   Pinto Points and Problems in Mojave Desert Archaeology. In *Anthropological Papers in Memory of Early H. Swanson, Jr.,* edited by L. B. Harten, C. N. Warren, and D. R. Tuohy, pp. 67–76. Special Publication of the Idaho Museum of Natural History, Pocatello.

1984   The Desert Region. In *California Archaeology*, edited by M. J. Moratto, pp. 339–430. Academic Press, Orlando, Florida.

Waters, M. R.
1986a Geoarchaeological Investigations of the Picacho Study Area. In *Prehistoric Hunter-Gatherers of South Central Arizona: The Picacho Reservoir Archaic Project*, edited by F. E. Bayham, D. H. Morris, and M. S. Shackley, pp. 17–35. Anthropological Field Studies No. 13. Office of Cultural Resource Management, Department of Anthropology, Arizona State University, Tempe.

1986b *The Geoarchaeology of Whitewater Draw, Arizona*. Anthropological Papers of the University of Arizona, Number 45. The University of Arizona Press, Tucson.

1996   *Surficial Geological Map of the Gila River Indian Community*. P-MIP Technical Report No. 96-1, Gila River Indian Community Cultural Resource Management Program, Sacaton.

Waters, M. R., and J. C. Ravesloot
2000   Late Quaternary Geology of the Middle Gila River, Gila River Indian Reservation, Arizona. *Quaternary Research* 54:49–57.

2001   Landscape Change and the Cultural Evolution of the Hohokam along the Middle Gila River and Other River Valleys in South-Central Arizona. *American Antiquity* 66(2):285–299.

Whittaker, J. C.
1984   *Arrowheads and Artisans: Stone Tool Manufacture and Individual Variation at Grasshopper Pueblo*. (Doctoral dissertation, University of Arizona). University Microfilms International, Ann Arbor

1987   Individual Variation as an Approach to Economic Organization: Projectile Points at Grasshopper Pueblo, Arizona. *Journal of Field Archaeology* 14:465–479.

1994   *Flintknapping: Making and Understanding Stone Tools*. 3rd edition. University of Texas Press, Austin.

Wilson, E. D.
1969   Mineral Deposits of the Gila River Indian Reservation, Arizona. Bulletin No. 179. Arizona Bureau of Mines, University of Arizona, Tucson.

Wilson, E. D., R. T. Moore, and J. R. Cooper
1969   *Geological Map of Arizona*. Arizona Bureau of Mines and United States Geological Survey, Reston, AZ.

APPENDIX A:
GRIC-CRMP PROJECTILE POINT ASSEMBLAGE

Appendix A: GRIC-CRMP Projectile Point Assemblage

Project	Task	Specimen	Site	Subspecimen	Material	Stage	Point Style	Comments
99.36	0	1	1194	1	Rhyolite	Completed	Cienega Stemmed	Well-made point.
99.18	0	6	931	1	Chert	Completed	Cienega Short	Possibly reworked for an arrow point, but stem is too wide.
97.26	1	7	460	1	Basalt	Completed	San Jose-Pinto B	Not a good example of San Jose-Pinto; possibly should be Teardrop style.
97.26	0	7	460	1	Basalt	Late Stage Preform	Indeterminate Large Point	
97.26	1	7	460	2	Rhyolite	Early Stage Preform	Indeterminate Large Point	Possibly for a small point--is very crude and poorly thinned. Numerous step fractures.
99.36	0	9	0	1	Rhyolite	Completed	Cienega Long	Well-made point.
97.26	1	10	460	1	Quartzite	Early Stage Preform	Indeterminate Large Point	
99.40	0	10	886	2	Chert	Early Stage Preform	Indeterminate Small Point	
97.34	0	12	911	1	Obsidian	Completed	U-shaped Base Triangular	
97.26	0	19	463	1	Chert	Early Stage Preform	Indeterminate Large Point	
2000.33	0	21	888	2	Quartzite	Early Stage Preform	Indeterminate Small Point	
97.33	0	21	782	1	Chalcedony	Early Stage Preform	Indeterminate Small Point	
94.14	0	24	363	1	Basalt	Completed	Indeterminate Large Point	Could be stemmed but more likely was corner-notched.
2000.33	0	26	888	1	Obsidian	Late Stage Preform	Intermediate Side-Notched	Possibly finished--very crude.
94.02	1	27	1112	1	Obsidian	Completed	Flanged	Possibly a drill but retouch angles are not correct.
97.29	1	30	915	1	Chert	Completed	Wide Side-Notched	
99.40	0	33	886	1	Basalt	Completed	U-shaped Base Triangular	Crude, possibly unfinished.
94.14	0	34	364	1	Quartzite	Completed	San Pedro	
97.26	0	34	0	1	Rhyolite	Completed	Gypsum	Strange material, possibly chert.
97.26	0	43	0	1	Basalt	Completed	Chiricahua	Both ears are broken.
2000.33	0	44	888	1	Obsidian	Completed	Straight Base Triangular	Heavily burned.
94.14	0	46	194	1	Chert	Completed	San Pedro	Shares some traits with Cienega points, and stem is narrower than most San Pedro points.

Continued

Appendix A: GRIC-CRMP Projectile Point Assemblage *(Continued)*

Project	Task	Specimen	Site	Subspecimen	Material	Stage	Point Style	Comments
2000.33	0	49	888	1	Obsidian	Completed	U-shaped Base Triangular	Deeply concave base--good example of the style.
99.40	0	51	887	1	Chert	Completed	Indeterminate Small Point	
97.26	0	53	0	1	Basalt	Completed	Stemmed Teardrop	Minimally retouched--teardrop-shaped.
97.26	0	54	0	1	Chert	Indeterminate	San Pedro	Edges are beveled and irregular; appears to be a reworked San Pedro point. The point possibly should be classified as stemmed.
2000.33	0	55	888	1	Chert	Early Stage Preform	Indeterminate Small Point	Unclear why this point wasn't finished--one edge isn't thinned.
99.40	0	59	887	1	Chert	Completed	San Pedro	Unusual material possibly not chert--could be rhyolite. Base is very slightly convex. Point is somewhat small for a San Pedro.
2000.33	0	60	888	2	Obsidian	Late Stage Preform	Indeterminate Small Point	Possibly finished.
97.26	0	64	456	1	Chalcedony	Completed	Cortaro	Possibly unfinished--point has a fracture running down the center--surprising that it didn't break. Highly crazed and appears heat-treated.
2000.33	0	74	888	1	Basalt	Late Stage Preform	Straight Base Triangular	Possibly finished but tip is irregular.
94.14	0	76	743	1	Obsidian	Completed	Intermediate Side-Notched	This is a reworked point tip that broke through the notches. Does not fit the typology well.
97.26	1	81	460	1	Meta-basalt	Completed	Indeterminate Large Point	Relatively small fragment, possibly from a small point.
97.29	1	82	915	1	Obsidian	Completed	Intermediate Side-Notched	Appears to have two side-notches on one margin.
97.26	0	83	0	1	Rhyolite	Completed	Indeterminate Large Point	Has deep and regular serrations.
97.26	4	83	660	1	Chert	Completed	San Pedro	Has pot-lid fractures-- has been heat-treated.
2000.03	0	84	1226	1	Obsidian	Early Stage Preform	U-shaped Base Triangular	
2000.33	0	84	888	1	Chert	Completed	Indeterminate Small Point	Possibly broke during notching.
97.26	1	85	460	1	Rhyolite	Late Stage Preform	Indeterminate Large Point	
94.14	0	90	375	1	Obsidian	Completed	U-shaped Base Triangular	Both ears missing--possibly unfinished (is rather thick).
99.40	0	92	891	1	Obsidian	Early Stage Preform	Indeterminate Small Point	

Continued

Appendix A: GRIC-CRMP Projectile Point Assemblage *(Continued)*

Project	Task	Specimen	Site	Subspecimen	Material	Stage	Point Style	Comments
97.26	0	93	0	1	Obsidian	Completed	Shouldered Teardrop	Possibly Government Mountain obsidian. Straight stemmed. Stem is somewhat narrow for a large point. Edges are irregular but does not appear intentionally serrated.
99.40	0	93	891	1	Chert	Late Stage Preform	Indeterminate	
2000.03	0	95	1226	1	Basalt	Late Stage Preform	Indeterminate Small Point	Possibly finished.
97.26	0	100	659	1	Basalt	Late Stage Preform	Indeterminate Small Point	
97.26	0	101	659	1	Quartz	Completed	Indeterminate Large Point	Possibly not a projectile point tip.
97.26	0	105	660	1	Basalt	Completed	Indeterminate	Very crude and minimal retouch.
2000.58	0	107	441	1	Obsidian	Completed	Straight Base Triangular	Possibly unfinished--minimal retouch.
2000.58	0	107	441	3	Chert	Early Stage Preform	Indeterminate Small Point	Possibly for a large point.
94.14	0	108	377	1	Chert	Late Stage Preform	Indeterminate Small Point	Possibly a large point preform but is too narrow.
97.26	0	109	660	1	Chalcedony	Early Stage Preform	Indeterminate Large Point	
94.14	0	115	378	1	Basalt	Early Stage Preform	Indeterminate Small Point	Possibly a very small large point.
97.26	0	122	660	1	Basalt	Early Stage Preform	Indeterminate Small Point	
2000.03	0	125	1228	1	Chert	Early Stage Preform	Indeterminate Small Point	
99.40	0	128	893	2	Obsidian	Completed	Intermediate Side-Notched	Was intensively burned after manufacture--possibly was in a cremation fire.
99.40	0	128	893	3	Obsidian	Completed	Intermediate Side-Notched	
94.14	0	129	380	1	Chert	Completed	Cortaro	Possibly unfinished but symmetrical and well thinned.
97.26	0	129	660	1	Chert	Late Stage Preform	Indeterminate Large Point	Too poorly made to call. Is possibly a crude large point.
99.40	0	131	893	1	Chalcedony	Completed	Eccentric	Unusual point--unique. Tip missing.
99.40	0	131	893	2	Chert	Completed	Indeterminate Small Point	Was intensively burned after manufacture--possibly was in a cremation fire.

Continued

Appendix A: GRIC-CRMP Projectile Point Assemblage *(Continued)*

Project	Task	Specimen	Site	Subspecimen	Material	Stage	Point Style	Comments
97.26	0	135	660	1	Chert	Early Stage Preform	Indeterminate Small Point	
2000.58	0	136	441	3	Chert	Completed	Indeterminate Small Point	Possibly a drill fragment but retouch angles are incorrect.
2000.58	0	136	441	2	Chert	Late Stage Preform	Indeterminate Small Point	
99.40	0	139	893	2	Basalt	Completed	U-shaped Base Triangular	Could be Straight Base triangular.
99.40	0	139	893	3	Obsidian	Completed	Intermediate Side-Notched	Very small.
99.40	0	139	893	4	Chert	Completed	Concave Blade	
99.40	0	141	893	1	Chert	Completed	San Jose-Pinto A	Has CaCO$_3$ encrustation. Clearly reused as a drill after it was originally made. Possibly unfinished.
99.40	0	146	894	2	Chert	Completed	Indeterminate Small Point	
99.40	0	146	894	3	Obsidian	Completed	Indeterminate Small Point	
99.40	0	146	894	5	Obsidian	Early Stage Preform	Indeterminate Small Point	
99.40	0	146	894	4	Obsidian	Early Stage Preform	Indeterminate Small Point	
99.40	0	149	894	2	Obsidian	Completed	Intermediate Side-Notched	
99.40	0	149	894	4	Obsidian	Completed	Indeterminate Small Point	
99.40	0	149	894	3	Chalcedony	Late Stage Preform	Indeterminate Small Point	Possibly finished.
94.14	0	153	383	1	Basalt	Completed	Indeterminate Large Point	Possibly small point fragment.
2000.03	0	160	1230	1	Rhyolite	Completed	Indeterminate Large Point	Possibly a knife.
99.40	0	160	894	2	Obsidian	Early Stage Preform	Flanged	Could be classified as side-notched.
98.02	0	165	932	1	Obsidian	Completed	Indeterminate Small Point	Doesn't fit the typology.
99.40	0	167	895	2	Obsidian	Completed	Indeterminate Small Point	

Continued

Appendix A: GRIC-CRMP Projectile Point Assemblage (Continued)

Project	Task	Specimen	Site	Subspecimen	Material	Stage	Point Style	Comments
98.02	0	177	934	1	Chert	Late Stage Preform	Indeterminate Small Point	Possibly finished but rather thick and irregular.
99.40	0	181	895	1	Obsidian	Completed	U-shaped Base Triangular	Very crude, possibly unfinished.
94.14	0	186	194	1	Rhyolite	Completed	Cienega Flared	Could be Cienega Long.
99.40	0	186	895	3	Obsidian	Completed	Intermediate Side-Notched	
99.40	0	186	895	4	Chalcedony	Completed	Concave Base Triangular	Well made point.
99.40	0	186	895	5	Chert	Completed	Wide Side-Notched	Possibly a large point.
99.40	0	186	895	6	Obsidian	Late Stage Preform	Intermediate Side-Notched	Appears to have broken during notching.
99.40	0	186	895	7	Obsidian	Completed	Indeterminate Small Point	
94.14	0	187	194	1	Meta-basalt	Early Stage Preform	Indeterminate Small Point	
2000.03	0	189	1234	1	Chert	Completed	U-shaped Base Triangular	Tip missing.
94.14	0	193	387	3	Quartz	Indeterminate	Indeterminate Small Point	Possibly a large point tip or a preform
94.14	0	193	387	4	Quartzite	Early Stage Preform	Indeterminate Small Point	
94.14	0	193	387	5	Chert	Completed	Middle Side-Notched	Tip and one ear missing.
99.40	0	195	895	2	Obsidian	Completed	Concave Blade	
99.40	0	195	895	3	Obsidian	Completed	Intermediate Side-Notched	
99.40	0	195	895	4	Rhyolite	Completed	Stemmed Teardrop	
94.14	0	200	320	1	Chert	Completed	U-shaped Base Triangular	One ear missing.
99.40	0	208	896	1	Obsidian	Completed	Indeterminate Small Point	
2000.03	0	209	909	1	Basalt	Completed	Concave Base Triangular	Possibly should be U-shaped Base Triangular.

Continued

Appendix A: GRIC-CRMP Projectile Point Assemblage (*Continued*)

Project	Task	Specimen	Site	Subspecimen	Material	Stage	Point Style	Comments
2000.03	0	210	909	1	Glass	Completed	U-shaped Base Triangular	One of the better-made glass points.
2000.03	0	211	909	1	Chert	Late Stage Preform	Indeterminate Large Point	Possibly a very crude completed point but lacks symmetry. Could be an early stage preform for a small point but is rather large. Is yellowish brown silicified wood.
2000.03	0	212	909	1	Basalt	Completed	Stemmed Teardrop	Very crude, possibly unfinished. Several major step fractures present.
2000.03	0	213	909	1	Basalt	Completed	Straight Base Triangular	
2000.03	0	214	909	1	Basalt	Completed	Straight Base Triangular	
2000.03	0	215	909	1	Basalt	Completed	U-shaped Base Triangular	Possibly should be Straight Base triangular.
2000.03	0	216	909	1	Basalt	Late Stage Preform	Indeterminate Small Point	
2000.03	0	217	909	1	Siltstone	Completed	Indeterminate Large Point	Too big for a small point but does not fit the large point typology.
97.26	1	220	460	1	Basalt	Completed	Shouldered Teardrop	Very crude and minimally retouched. Possibly could be forced into the San Jose-Pinto style.
2000.03	0	222	909	1	Basalt	Early Stage Preform	Indeterminate Small Point	
97.26	0	224	664	1	Chert	Completed	Cortaro	Very possibly unfinished--has a trimmed base and may be a corner-notched point preform.
2000.03	0	230	909	1	Obsidian	Completed	U-shaped Base Triangular	
94.14	0	230	390	1	Chalcedony	Late Stage Preform	Indeterminate Small Point	Possibly a crude finished point (U-shaped Base Triangular).
97.26	0	236	665	1	Chert	Completed	San Jose-Pinto A	The very tip and one ear are missing. Has relatively deep serrations.
94.14	0	237	1073	4	Quartzite	Completed	Indeterminate Large Point	Very crude, possibly unfinished but is fairly regularly shaped. Similar to teardrop shaped styles.
97.26	0	237	665	1	Basalt	Completed	San Jose-Pinto A	Small for a Pinto. At the lower size limit for dart points.
97.26	0	238	665	1	Basalt	Completed	San Jose-Pinto A	Pretty good example of San Jose. Has weakly serrated edges.
97.26	1	238	460	1	Basalt	Completed	San Jose-Pinto A	Very crude point, difficult to type.
97.26	0	239	665	1	Rhyolite	Early Stage Preform	Indeterminate Large Point	Has 2 step fractures and is twisted--probably broken during manufacture.
94.02	1	240	1112	1	Basalt	Completed	Flanged	Doesn't fit the typology well.

Continued

Appendix A: GRIC-CRMP Projectile Point Assemblage (Continued)

Project	Task	Specimen	Site	Subspecimen	Material	Stage	Point Style	Comments
97.26	0	240	665	1	Quartzite	Completed	Stemmed Shouldered	Poorly thinned. Edges are irregular, possibly serrated. Teardrop shaped. Base appears broken but could be a very short stem.
97.26	0	241	665	1	Obsidian	Completed	Indeterminate	Very crude point. Small point size but shares some similarities with San Jose points collected in the area. Curved and poorly thinned. Appears highly weathered--the entire artifact has a frosted appearance--looks sand-blasted.
97.26	0	242	665	1	Obsidian	Completed	Indeterminate Large Point	Highly weathered obsidian. Very small point, possibly a Pinto but has been reworked (the tip appears truncated). Possibly should be classified as a small point.
97.26	0	243	665	1	Basalt	Completed	San Jose-Pinto B	Very long and well-thinned point.
97.26	0	244	665	1	Quartz	Completed	San Pedro	Very small, appears to be a reworked San Pedro but the stem is a little narrow.
97.26	0	245	665	1	Basalt	Completed	San Jose-Pinto A	Stem is very slightly expanding. Possibly not a San Jose-Pinto. This point shares some similarities with the Bajada style, but the shoulders are not as prominent.
94.14	0	248	344	1	Chert	Early Stage Preform	Indeterminate Large Point	May not have usewear. Large step fracture precluded further thinning--the artifact also has an irregular outline suggesting it is unfinished.
2000.03	0	250	909	1	Basalt	Completed	Straight Base Triangular	Possibly unfinished.
97.26	0	250	665	1	Basalt	Completed	Indeterminate	Very crude--minimally retouched--possibly for a small point.
2000.03	0	251	909	1	Basalt	Completed	U-shaped Base Triangular	Possibly should be Straight Base Triangular.
94.14	0	251	493	1	Basalt	Completed	Long Triangular	Possibly unfinished. Has cortex on both faces.
2000.03	0	252	909	1	Basalt	Completed	Straight Base Triangular	Possibly U-shaped Base Triangular
94.14	0	252	493	2	Obsidian	Completed	U-shaped Base Triangular	Could be Concave Base Triangular.
2000.03	0	253	909	1	Basalt	Completed	Straight Base Triangular	
2000.03	0	254	909	1	Basalt	Late Stage Preform	Indeterminate Small Point	
94.14	0	254	493	1	Obsidian	Completed	Intermediate Side-Notched	
2000.03	0	255	909	1	Basalt	Completed	Long Triangular	
97.26	0	257	665	1	Basalt	Early Stage Preform	Indeterminate Large Point	
2000.03	0	258	909	1	Quartzite	Completed	Straight Base Triangular	Possibly unfinished-- crude.
94.14	0	258	231	1	Obsidian	Completed	Indeterminate Small Point	Very crude with minimal retouch.

Continued

Appendix A: GRIC-CRMP Projectile Point Assemblage *(Continued)*

Project	Task	Specimen	Site	Subspecimen	Material	Stage	Point Style	Comments
94.14	0	258	493	1	Chert	Completed	Indeterminate Small Point	
94.14	0	258	231	2	Chert	Completed	U-shaped Base Triangular	
2000.03	0	259	909	1	Basalt	Completed	Straight Base Triangular	Crude--possibly unfinished.
94.14	0	267	231	1	Rhyolite	Completed	Cortaro	Quite possibly unfinished but has regular edges and is fairly well thinned.
97.26	0	271	666	1	Basalt	Early Stage Preform	Indeterminate Large Point	Very early stage preform.
97.26	4	272	660	1	Chert	Completed	San Jose-Pinto A	Possibly unfinished. Has several step fractures on each face but has a fairly regular outline.
97.26	0	275	665	1	Basalt	Completed	San Jose-Pinto A	Appears to have a long and straight stem, but the point may lack shoulders (no stem separate from the blade).
99.40	0	276	832	1	Chert	Late Stage Preform	Indeterminate Small Point	Possibly large point preform but is narrow.
94.14	0	283	233	1	Chert	Completed	Indeterminate Small Point	Probably from an U-shaped Base Triangular style pt.
94.14	0	283	233	2	Chert	Completed	U-shaped Base Triangular	Both ears and tip missing.
94.14	0	286	347	1	Obsidian	Early Stage Preform	Indeterminate Small Point	Very crude; appears to be an early stage preform.
2000.03	0	288	909	1	Chert	Early Stage Preform	Indeterminate	Appears to be a bifacially reduced small core that was partially thinned into a point preform, but is possibly only a core.
94.14	0	290	225	1	Obsidian	Early Stage Preform	Indeterminate Small Point	
94.14	0	290	347	1	Chalcedony	Early Stage Preform	Indeterminate Small Point	Possibly for a large point. Has large step fracture (probably why it was discarded).
94.14	0	292	347	2	Chert	Early Stage Preform	Indeterminate Small Point	
98.02	0	294	1057	1	Chalcedony	Completed	Intermediate Side-Notched	
94.14	0	295	495	1	Basalt	Completed	Straight Base Triangular	Very crude, possibly unfinished.
97.26	0	295	667	1	Chert	Completed	Indeterminate Large Point	Has thick CaCO$_3$ adhering. Possibly a small point. Too fragmentary to classify.
94.14	0	296	495	1	Basalt	Late Stage Preform	U-shaped Base Triangular	Possibly finished.

Continued

Appendix A: GRIC-CRMP Projectile Point Assemblage *(Continued)*

Project	Task	Specimen	Site	Subspecimen	Material	Stage	Point Style	Comments
94.02	1	298	1112	1	Quartz	Completed	Indeterminate Small Point	
94.14	0	301	349	3	Chert	Completed	Cortaro	Possibly unfinished. Step fractures on one margin but otherwise well made. Large scars thinned with a soft hammer. Material is silicified wood.
94.14	0	301	349	1	Chert	Completed	Cortaro	Possibly unfinished--has one step fracture but point is otherwise well thinned and symmetrical. Material is silicified wood.
94.14	0	303	195	1	Basalt	Completed	U-shaped Base Triangular	Possibly Straight Base Triangular.
94.14	0	311	235	1	Obsidian	Completed	U-shaped Base Triangular	Very crude; possibly unfinished; could be Straight Base Triangular; possibly glass.
97.26	4	312	660	1	Rhyolite	Completed	Indeterminate Large Point	
97.26	0	314	669	1	Basalt	Completed	Indeterminate Large Point	Possibly a small point. Unusual style with relatively wide serrations.
97.26	0	315	669	1	Basalt	Completed	San Jose-Pinto A	Could be called side- or corner-notched. Stem is a little narrow for San Jose.
2000.03	0	317	909	1	Rhyolite	Completed	Straight Base Triangular	Possibly unfinished, minimally retouched.
97.26	0	319	0	1	Obsidian	Early Stage Preform	Indeterminate Large Point	Size suggests this is a small point preform, but the obsidian is highly weathered suggesting great antiquity.
97.26	0	322	670	1	Chert	Completed	Intermediate Side-Notched	Possibly a Chiricahua point but is a little small. Tip is burinated on both edges. Has a deeply concave base. The stem width is just above the cut-off for arrow points but is very thin for a dart point.
2000.03	0	332	909	1	Basalt	Early Stage Preform	Indeterminate Large Point	Possibly a small point preform.
97.26	0	339	1242	1	Chert	Completed	Cienega Short	Very crude little point--possibly not reworked.
97.26	0	340	1242	1	Quartzite	Completed	San Jose-Pinto A	Blade margins are only slightly convex.
97.26	0	342	1242	1	Obsidian	Completed	Intermediate Side-Notched	Highly fragmentary--style may be wrong.
97.26	0	343	1242	1	Meta-basalt	Completed	Indeterminate Large Point	Crude, possibly unfinished.
94.14	0	345	191	1	Chert	Indeterminate	Indeterminate Large Point	Appears heat treated. Possibly a small point preform--thickness suggests that it is a large point
94.14	0	346	1188	1	Chert	Completed	San Jose-Pinto A	Possibly a small point but appears to be a reworked Archaic point. A light patina covers the reworked area suggesting the point was reworked not long after manufacture. Does not fit the typology.
94.14	0	347	1188	1	Obsidian	Completed	San Jose-Pinto A	

Continued

Appendix A: GRIC-CRMP Projectile Point Assemblage *(Continued)*

Project	Task	Specimen	Site	Subspecimen	Material	Stage	Point Style	Comments
97.26	0	347	1242	1	Chert	Late Stage Preform	Indeterminate Large Point	
97.26	0	348	1242	1	Rhyolite	Early Stage Preform	Indeterminate Large Point	
97.26	0	349	1242	1	Basalt	Completed	Stemmed Teardrop	
94.02	1	351	1112	1	Obsidian	Completed	Intermediate Side-Notched	Doesn't fit the typology well.
94.14	0	351	237	3	Chert	Completed	San Pedro	The point is possibly not a San Pedro but is definitely a large point style. Reworking is suggested by flakes that originate on the edge of a snap fracture through the notches.
94.14	0	351	237	4	Chert	Completed	U-shaped Base Triangular	
94.14	0	351	237	1	Chert	Completed	U-shaped Base Triangular	Could be a fragment from a large point--style may be wrong
94.14	0	352	1188	1	Basalt	Completed	San Jose-Pinto A	
94.14	0	353	1188	1	Chert	Completed	Chiricahua	Looks like a small point style but is too large and has comparatively heavy patina. Much better made and larger than most Chiricahua points.
2000.03	0	358	909	1	Basalt	Late Stage Preform	Indeterminate Small Point	
94.14	0	358	355	2	Chert	Completed	U-shaped Base Triangular	Very fine serrations. Large for a U-shaped Base Triangular point.
94.14	0	358	355	3	Rhyolite	Completed	Cortaro	Very good possibility this is a preform that broke during manufacture. One blade margin isn't straight (appears unfinished), and the break is along a step fracture.
94.14	0	358	355	4	Chert	Late Stage Preform	U-shaped Base Triangular	Crude--possibly unfinished.
94.14	0	360	1190	1	Basalt	Completed	San Jose-Pinto A	Heavy CaCO₃ encrustation. Appears to have been reworked shortly after time of manufacture.
2000.03	0	361	909	1	Rhyolite	Early Stage Preform	Indeterminate	Has bifacil thinning--possibly a small fragment from a larger biface that was reworked but may have been a flake.
94.14	0	361	1190	1	Rhyolite	Completed	Chiricahua	Possibly reworked into a small point.
97.26	0	361	1243	1	Basalt	Completed	Stemmed Teardrop	Quite possibly unfinished. Has poorly defined stem.
94.14	0	362	470	1	Basalt	Completed	San Jose-Pinto A	Does not fit typology well.
2000.03	0	363	909	1	Basalt	Completed	Straight Base Triangular	Possibly rhyolite. Could be unfinished.

Appendix A: GRIC-CRMP Projectile Point Assemblage (Continued)

Project	Task	Specimen	Site	Subspecimen	Material	Stage	Point Style	Comments
97.26	0	363	1243	1	Chert	Completed	Chiricahua	Possibly reworked.
97.26	0	364	1243	1	Basalt	Completed	Indeterminate Large Point	
94.14	0	365	355	1	Chert	Late Stage Preform	Cortaro	Probably a preform that broke during manufacture.
97.26	0	365	1243	1	Basalt	Completed	Cienega Stemmed	Is arrow point sized.
94.14	0	366	355	2	Basalt	Completed	Indeterminate Large Point	Very strange artifact. Is ground on both faces, and is possibly a drill but lacks wear on tip. The point is shaped like a diamond. Possibly could be a small point.
94.14	0	369	1191	1	Basalt	Completed	San Pedro	Not a very good example of a San Pedro point.
94.14	0	370	1191	1	Basalt	Completed	Shouldered Teardrop	Point is possibly a small point style.
94.14	0	376	237	1	Chert	Completed	U-shaped Base Triangular	Large (wide) for an U-shaped Base Triangular point and lacks serration.
94.14	0	376	1191	1	Rhyolite	Early Stage Preform	Indeterminate Large Point	Early stage preform probably for a large point.
94.02	1	377	1112	1	Obsidian	Completed	Middle Side-Notched	
94.14	0	377	1191	1	Basalt	Completed	Stemmed Teardrop	Does not fit typology well. Has convex edges and sloping shoulders.
97.26	0	378	0	1	Chert	Completed	Chiricahua	Very bad example of Chiricahua--possibly shouldn't be included. Possibly not finished as it has hinge fractures and is rather thick.
97.26	0	387	0	1	Basalt	Completed	Chiricahua	Crude and possibly unfinished.
97.26	0	388	0	1	Obsidian	Completed	Cienega Short	Tip of point was clearly reworked.
2000.03	0	389	909	1	Chalcedony	Completed	Straight Base Triangular	Possibly unfinished--minimally retouched.
2000.03	0	390	909	1	Quartz	Completed	Gypsum	Smaller than most Gypsum points and lacks abrupt shoulders.
2000.03	0	393	909	1	Basalt	Completed	U-shaped Base Triangular	Could be Concave base, but base is only moderately concave.
94.14	0	395	237	1	Chert	Early Stage Preform	Indeterminate Small Point	
2000.03	0	399	909	1	Meta-basalt	Completed	San Pedro	Very crude, possibly unfinished but is notched. Has a large isolated mass on one face making it quite thick. Blade margins are irregular but don't appear intentionally serrated. Possibly a San Jose-Pinto..
94.14	0	404	237	1	Chert	Early Stage Preform	Indeterminate Small Point	Minimal retouch.
94.02	1	422	1112	1	Chalcedony	Completed	Long Triangular	Possibly unfinished, very crude.

Continued

Appendix A: GRIC-CRMP Projectile Point Assemblage (*Continued*)

Project	Task	Specimen	Site	Subspecimen	Material	Stage	Point Style	Comments
2000.03	0	426	909	1	Basalt	Completed	U-shaped Base Triangular	Base is only moderately concave--could be Straight Base Triangular.
2000.03	0	427	909	1	Basalt	Completed	U-shaped Base Triangular	
94.14	0	433	441	2	Obsidian	Completed	Indeterminate Small Point	Appears to be the base of a reworked point. Tip is missing.
2000.58	1	434	441	1	Chert	Completed	Flanged	Appears to have been burned after manufacture.
94.02	1	434	1112	1	Obsidian	Completed	Concave Blade	
97.26	0	438	1247	1	Chert	Completed	San Pedro	Not a good example of San Pedro.
94.14	0	439	441	2	Chert	Completed	Wide Side-Notched	Doesn't fit the typology well. Has very wide notches, the point is thick and the notches may have been an attempt to thin the base.
94.14	0	439	441	4	Chert	Completed	Stemmed Tanged	
94.14	0	439	774	1	Rhyolite	Completed	San Pedro	As with most San Pedro points one shoulder is abrupt and one is sloping. Notches are lower than usual.
94.14	0	446	1192	1	Chert	Late Stage Preform	Indeterminate Small Point	
94.14	0	448	236	1	Chert	Indeterminate	U-shaped Base Triangular	Wider than most U-shaped Base Triangular points.
97.26	0	448	1247	1	Basalt	Completed	San Jose-Pinto B	Very crude. Quite possibly unfinished.
97.26	0	449	1247	1	Basalt	Completed	Cienega Long	Possibly a Cienega Short.
97.26	4	450	660	1	Obsidian	Early Stage Preform	Indeterminate Small Point	
2000.03	0	455	909	1	Basalt	Completed	U-shaped Base Triangular	Between a Straight Base Triangular and U-shaped Base Triangular.
2000.03	0	456	909	1	Chert	Late Stage Preform	Indeterminate Small Point	Possibly finished but base is only partially thinned & edges are irregular
97.26	0	458	0	1	Chert	Completed	Straight Base Triangular	Appears to have been used as a perforator.
94.14	0	459	1193	1	Welded Tuff	Late Stage Preform	Indeterminate Large Point	Has step fractures and isolated mass.
97.26	0	459	0	1	Chert	Early Stage Preform	Indeterminate Small Point	Unusual double notches.
97.26	4	459	660	1	Basalt	Late Stage Preform	Indeterminate Large Point	
94.14	0	460	1193	1	Chert	Early Stage Preform	Indeterminate Large Point	Possibly for a small point. Base is trimmed (possibly a stage in the production of corner-notched points) but is a little thin for a large point. Has step fractures on the opposing faces along one edge--bad news for further thinning.

Continued

Appendix A: GRIC-CRMP Projectile Point Assemblage (*Continued*)

Project	Task	Specimen	Site	Subspecimen	Material	Stage	Point Style	Comments
97.26	0	460	1250	1	Basalt	Completed	Shouldered Teardrop	Possibly should be Gypsum.
97.26	0	461	1250	1	Basalt	Completed	Cienega Long	
97.26	0	462	1250	1	Chert	Completed	Cienega Stemmed	Well-made point and nearly complete.
2000.03	0	463	909	1	Obsidian	Completed	U-shaped Base Triangular	Possibly Straight Base Triangular.
97.26	0	463	1250	1	Chert	Completed	Shouldered Teardrop	Possibly reworked but no obvious evidence.
2000.03	0	464	909	1	Chert	Completed	U-shaped Base Triangular	Possibly unfinished. Could be Straight Base Triangular.
97.26	0	464	1250	1	Chert	Completed	Cienega Long	Well-made point.
2000.03	0	465	909	1	Basalt	Completed	Long Triangular	
2000.03	0	466	909	1	Chalcedony	Completed	U-shaped Base Triangular	
2000.03	0	471	909	1	Basalt	Completed	Indeterminate Small Point	
94.14	0	472	1195	1	Chert	Completed	Intermediate Side-Notched	Unusual point--stem is rather wide for an arrow point. Very deeply concave base. Does not fit typology well.
94.14	0	478	1196	1	Chert	Completed	U-shaped Base Triangular	
94.14	0	484	1196	1	Basalt	Completed	Cienega Short	Could be a small point style but appears to be a point tip that was reworked into a Cienega Short.
2000.03	0	485	909	1	Meta-basalt	Late Stage Preform	Indeterminate Small Point	
2000.03	0	486	909	1	Basalt	Completed	Long Triangular	
2000.03	0	487	909	1	Chert	Late Stage Preform	Indeterminate Small Point	
2000.58	1	489	441	2	Chert	Completed	Cienega Stemmed	Very good example of this style.
94.14	0	489	196	1	Basalt	Completed	San Jose-Pinto A	Point appears to have been reused as a drill.
94.14	0	489	194	1	Siltstone	Completed	Cienega Long	Very well made point. Neck and base are wider than most Cienega points.
2000.03	0	491	909	1	Basalt	Completed	Long Triangular	
94.14	0	492	1151	1	Glass	Completed	U-shaped Base Triangular	Very thick--possibly unfinished. Rather large for an U-shaped Base Triangular point
97.26	0	492	1252	1	Obsidian	Completed	Intermediate Side-Notched	Appears to have a basal notch.

Continued

Appendix A: GRIC-CRMP Projectile Point Assemblage *(Continued)*

Project	Task	Specimen	Site	Subspecimen	Material	Stage	Point Style	Comments
99.18	2	492	931	1	Chert	Completed	Straight Base Triangular	
2000.03	0	493	909	2	Obsidian	Completed	Straight Base Triangular	
94.02	1	499	1112	1	Chert	Completed	Narrow Side-Notched	
94.14	0	499	1197	1	Basalt	Completed	Indeterminate Large Point	Does not fit the typology. Fresh breaks at middle and shoulder. Somewhat similar to Elko Corner-Notched style. Quite wide point that is very well made.
97.26	0	499	1252	1	Basalt	Completed	Shouldered Teardrop	Very crude point.
94.14	0	501	196	1	Basalt	Completed	Silver Lake	Point does not fit into the typology well. Possibly a Gypsum. Crudely made. Appears to have been reworked.
97.26	0	501	1252	1	Basalt	Completed	Indeterminate Large Point	
2000.03	0	502	909	1	Chalcedony	Completed	Straight Base Triangular	
94.14	0	502	700	1	Chert	Completed	Flanged	Possibly unfinished.
97.26	0	502	1252	1	Rhyolite	Late Stage Preform	Indeterminate Large Point	
94.02	1	508	1112	1	Chert	Completed	Concave Blade	Quite possibly a more recent style.
97.26	0	512	1252	1	Rhyolite	Completed	Indeterminate Large Point	A little thin for a large point. Possibly a San Jose midsection but too fragmentary to classify.
94.14	0	513	702	1	Quartzite	Early Stage Preform	Indeterminate Large Point	Very early stage preform.
97.26	0	513	1252	1	Rhyolite	Late Stage Preform	Indeterminate Large Point	
97.26	0	514	1252	1	Dacite	Completed	Gypsum	Fairly good example of Gypsum.
97.26	0	515	1252	1	Rhyolite	Completed	Indeterminate Small Point	
94.14	0	516	402	1	Chert	Completed	Indeterminate Large Point	Well made. One edge is burinated (probably accidentally).
94.14	0	517	703	1	Basalt	Early Stage Preform	Indeterminate Large Point	Very crude small biface.
94.14	0	524	194	1	Basalt	Completed	Gypsum	Good example of Gypsum.
94.14	0	524	704	1	Chalcedony	Late Stage Preform	Indeterminate Small Point	

Continued

Appendix A: GRIC-CRMP Projectile Point Assemblage (*Continued*)

Project	Task	Specimen	Site	Subspecimen	Material	Stage	Point Style	Comments
2000.03	0	526	1235	1	Glass	Completed	U-shaped Base Triangular	Fairly well made glass point.
94.14	0	530	704	1	Basalt	Late Stage Preform	Gypsum	Not a good example of Gypsum. Possibly a crude completed point but was probably discarded late in the manufacturing sequence due to step fractures.
94.14	0	531	704	1	Chert	Late Stage Preform	Indeterminate Small Point	
2000.03	0	533	1235	1	Basalt	Completed	Concave Base Triangular	Possibly unfinished, somewhat crude.
94.14	0	536	705	1	Chert	Completed	U-shaped Base Triangular	Poorly made, possibly unfinished.
94.14	0	537	1057	1	Chalcedony	Completed	Indeterminate Small Point	Probably a side-notched point of some type.
2000.03	0	541	909	1	Basalt	Completed	U-shaped Base Triangular	
94.14	0	546	689	1	Quartz	Early Stage Preform	Indeterminate Small Point	
94.14	0	552	1057	1	Obsidian	Completed	Concave Blade	
94.14	0	554	191	1	Basalt	Completed	Indeterminate Large Point	Very well made. Regular and deep serrations. Does not fit typology.
94.14	0	557	251	1	Chert	Late Stage Preform	Indeterminate Large Point	Possibly a knife.
2000.03	0	559	909	1	Chert	Completed	Indeterminate Small Point	
94.14	0	559	194	1	Siltstone	Completed	San Pedro	Has a concave base--possibly damaged. Not a good example of San Pedro.
94.14	0	560	194	1	Basalt	Completed	Chiricahua	Point is possibly reworked.
94.14	0	562	194	1	Basalt	Completed	San Jose-Pinto B	Good example of a San Jose.
94.02	1	564	1112	1	Chert	Completed	Chiricahua	Possibly small point, broken through the notches is narrow.
94.14	0	568	691	1	Obsidian	Completed	Indeterminate	Unusual point with deep serrations. Base is broken, could have had very wide side-notches or a stem. The neck is very thick suggesting a dart point, but the neck width suggests an arrow point.
94.14	0	572	191	1	Chert	Early Stage Preform	Indeterminate Large Point	Possibly for a small point. Minimal retouch resulted in unusual shape.
94.14	0	575	409	1	Chert	Completed	Indeterminate Small Point	
2000.03	0	581	909	1	Chalcedony	Completed	U-shaped Base Triangular	

Continued

Appendix A: GRIC-CRMP Projectile Point Assemblage *(Continued)*

Project	Task	Specimen	Site	Subspecimen	Material	Stage	Point Style	Comments
94.14	0	581	692	1	Basalt	Completed	Indeterminate Large Point	Possibly a late prehistoric spear point. Too fragmentary to tell.
2000.03	0	582	909	1	Rhyolite	Completed	U-shaped Base Triangular	
2000.03	0	583	909	1	Obsidian	Completed	U-shaped Base Triangular	
2000.03	0	584	909	1	Obsidian	Late Stage Preform	Indeterminate Small Point	
94.14	0	590	693	1	Welded Tuff	Completed	Indeterminate Large Point	Possibly the tip of a Cienega Long or Flared.
94.14	0	591	717	1	Quartz	Completed	Indeterminate Small Point	Doesn't fit typology. Possibly Stemmed Barbed or Stemmed Tanged.
94.14	0	595	1057	1	Obsidian	Completed	Intermediate Side-Notched	Appears to be a reworked point tip
94.14	0	595	413	3	Chert	Completed	Cortaro	Possibly a preform or a knife. Heat-treated--point broke along a pot-lid fracture.
94.14	0	606	688	1	Basalt	Completed	Cienega Long	Style is possibly incorrect given that the base is missing.
94.14	0	607	1057	1	Obsidian	Completed	Concave Blade	Point is ground.
94.14	0	611	1121	1	Chert	Completed	Flanged	This is probably a reworked Archaic point. The base appears to be on a snap fracture. The point flares at the base.
2000.03	0	612	909	1	Basalt	Completed	Mojave Lake	Possibly unfinished.
94.14	0	613	191	1	Chert	Late Stage Preform	Indeterminate Large Point	
94.14	0	615	191	1	Chert	Completed	Indeterminate Small Point	
94.14	0	616	191	1	Obsidian	Completed	U-shaped Base Triangular	Government Mountain obsidian. Tip possibly broken.
94.14	0	616	254	1	Chert	Late Stage Preform	Cortaro	Made from silicified wood--possibly a completed unnotched large point.
94.14	0	621	722	1	Chert	Completed	U-shaped Base Triangular	
94.14	0	622	722	1	Chert	Indeterminate	Indeterminate	
94.14	0	623	722	1	Chert	Completed	U-shaped Base Triangular	
94.14	0	625	722	2	Basalt	Completed	Indeterminate Large Point	Very crude point, quite possibly unfinished.

Continued

Appendix A: GRIC-CRMP Projectile Point Assemblage *(Continued)*

Project	Task	Specimen	Site	Subspecimen	Material	Stage	Point Style	Comments
2000.03	0	629	909	1	Basalt	Late Stage Preform	Indeterminate	Very heavy wear, possibly not a projectile point, but size (other than thickness) and shape are correct for a small point. Appears to be a preform that was intensively used rather than discarded.
94.14	0	639	814	1	Basalt	Completed	Cienega Short	Poorly made. Possibly unfinished. Could be a Cienega or Gypsum point. Probably Late Archaic because it is small. Maybe arrow point sized.
2000.03	0	642	909	2	Glass	Late Stage Preform	Indeterminate Small Point	Very crude. Possibly a very poorly made finished point but is rather thick.
94.14	0	644	1057	1	Obsidian	Late Stage Preform	Intermediate Side-Notched	Possibly unfinished, base is minimally retouched and broken (may have broken during manufacture).
94.14	0	644	722	1	Chert	Completed	Indeterminate Large Point	Possibly for a small point.
2000.03	0	647	909	1	Chert	Early Stage Preform	Straight Base Triangular	Possibly unfinished--very crude.
2000.03	0	649	909	1	Chert	Early Stage Preform	Indeterminate Small Point	
2000.03	0	650	909	1	Obsidian	Completed	U-shaped Base Triangular	Very crude, possibly unfinished.
2000.03	0	651	909	1	Obsidian	Completed	U-shaped Base Triangular	Very crude, may not be finished.
94.14	0	657	815	1	Obsidian	Completed	U-shaped Base Triangular	
2000.03	0	665	1236	1	Chert	Early Stage Preform	Indeterminate Small Point	Possibly finished but very thick. Unusual pink material.
94.14	0	665	726	1	Obsidian	Late Stage Preform	Indeterminate Small Point	
94.14	0	669	727	1	Chert	Completed	U-shaped Base Triangular	
94.14	0	670	727	1	Chert	Completed	U-shaped Base Triangular	
2000.03	0	672	1237	1	Chert	Completed	Indeterminate Small Point	Possibly not finished but is serrated. A little large--possibly could be Cienega Stemmed.
94.14	0	677	728	1	Chert	Late Stage Preform	Indeterminate Small Point	Possibly finished but very crude.
94.14	0	681	931	1	Chert	Completed	Indeterminate Small Point	
94.14	0	687	1057	1	Obsidian	Late Stage Preform	Intermediate Side-Notched	Base is broken and has unusual fracture along edge.

Continued

Appendix A: GRIC-CRMP Projectile Point Assemblage *(Continued)*

Project	Task	Specimen	Site	Subspecimen	Material	Stage	Point Style	Comments
94.14	0	687	931	1	Obsidian	Completed	Concave Base Triangular	Possibly U-shaped Base Triangular.
94.14	0	687	728	1	Chert	Late Stage Preform	Indeterminate Small Point	Is not thinned on one edge, clearly a preform.
94.14	0	687	728	2	Chert	Late Stage Preform	Indeterminate Small Point	Possibly for a large point.
94.14	0	688	728	1	Chert	Late Stage Preform	Indeterminate Small Point	Unclear why this was not finished.
94.14	0	688	931	1	Chert	Completed	Indeterminate Large Point	
94.14	0	689	931	1	Chert	Late Stage Preform	Indeterminate Small Point	
2000.03	0	691	909	1	Basalt	Completed	Straight Base Triangular	Possibly should be U-shaped Base Triangular but lacks notching and the base is not highly concave.
94.14	0	693	816	1	Chert	Completed	Concave Blade	
2000.03	0	701	909	1	Chert	Completed	Indeterminate Large Point	Unusually deep and wide serrations. Material may be rhyolite rather than chert. The point is broken above the hafting element and the type is unclear; it was more than 52 mm in length.
94.14	0	703	421	1	Chert	Completed	Middle Side-Notched	
94.02	1	719	1112	2	Obsidian	Completed	Indeterminate Small Point	Possibly unfinished.
94.14	0	720	731	1	Chert	Completed	Long Triangular	
94.14	0	721	421	1	Basalt	Early Stage Preform	Indeterminate Large Point	Possibly crude bifacial knife fragment.
2000.03	0	723	909	1	Basalt	Completed	U-shaped Base Triangular	Possibly should be Concave Base Triangular or Bulbous Base--doesn't fit the typology well.
94.14	0	724	1057	1	Chalcedony	Late Stage Preform	Indeterminate Small Point	
94.14	0	724	1057	2	Chert	Indeterminate	Indeterminate Small Point	Possibly Concave Blade but is too small to tell.
94.14	0	728	1057	1	Chalcedony	Completed	Concave Blade	
94.14	0	728	821	1	Basalt	Completed	Indeterminate Small Point	Very crude. Quite possibly unfinished. Could be a large point.
2000.03	0	729	909	1	Basalt	Early Stage Preform	Indeterminate Small Point	

Continued

Appendix A: GRIC-CRMP Projectile Point Assemblage (Continued)

Project	Task	Specimen	Site	Subspecimen	Material	Stage	Point Style	Comments
2000.03	0	729	909	2	Basalt	Completed	Straight Base Triangular	Slightly concave base.
94.14	0	733	256	2	Chert	Completed	U-shaped Base Triangular	Very good example of style, missing one ear.
2000.03	0	737	909	1	Obsidian	Completed	Straight Base Triangular	
2000.03	0	738	909	1	Obsidian	Completed	Straight Base Triangular	Possibly glass.
2000.03	0	741	909	1	Basalt	Completed	Straight Base Triangular	Slightly concave base.
94.14	0	743	1197	1	Basalt	Completed	Cortaro	Possibly a small unnotched point--is on the small/large point cusp.
94.14	0	749	441	2	Obsidian	Early Stage Preform	Indeterminate Small Point	
94.14	0	749	441	3	Obsidian	Early Stage Preform	Indeterminate Small Point	Very crude. Has notches but almost certainly isn't a finished (i.e., functional) point.
2000.03	0	750	909	2	Chert	Late Stage Preform	Indeterminate Small Point	
94.14	0	754	766	1	Chert	Completed	Intermediate Side-Notched	Tip appears to have broken and then been reworked.
94.14	0	757	1198	1	Chert	Late Stage Preform	Indeterminate Small Point	Edge angles prevented further thinning--clearly a preform.
2000.03	0	760	909	1	Chert	Completed	U-shaped Base Triangular	
94.14	0	762	766	1	Chalcedony	Completed	Indeterminate Small Point	
94.14	0	762	1198	1	Chert	Late Stage Preform	Indeterminate Large Point	Apparently discarded due to step fracture on one edge, but recovery might have been possible. It possibly broke during thinning, but recovery of both pieces is not probable.
94.14	0	766	1057	1	Chert	Completed	Concave Blade	
94.14	0	768	423	1	Obsidian	Completed	Intermediate Side-Notched	Well made
94.14	0	768	423	2	Chert	Early Stage Preform	Indeterminate Large Point	Early stage preform fragment.
94.14	0	776	1198	1	Chert	Early Stage Preform	Indeterminate Small Point	
94.14	0	776	1198	2	Rhyolite	Early Stage Preform	Indeterminate Small Point	Possibly for a large point.

Continued

Appendix A: GRIC-CRMP Projectile Point Assemblage *(Continued)*

Project	Task	Specimen	Site	Subspecimen	Material	Stage	Point Style	Comments
2000.03	0	777	909	1	Basalt	Late Stage Preform	Indeterminate Small Point	Has step fractures and isolated mass.
2000.03	0	778	909	1	Basalt	Late Stage Preform	Indeterminate Small Point	Possibly a crude finished point.
94.14	0	778	1198	1	Chert	Early Stage Preform	Indeterminate	Part of a large or small point preform.
2000.03	0	779	909	1	Basalt	Completed	Cienega Long	Tip is possibly reworked or unfinished. Fairly good example of the Cienega style.
94.14	0	795	744	1	Basalt	Completed	Straight Base Triangular	Possibly unfinished, Base slightly concave. Could be U-shaped Base Triangular.
94.14	0	797	744	1	Chert	Completed	Concave Blade	
94.14	0	798	1057	1	Chert	Completed	Indeterminate Large Point	Has been heat-treated (crazing and pot-lids present), possibly after it was made.
2000.03	0	799	909	1	Basalt	Early Stage Preform	Indeterminate Large Point	This preform has clearly been reworked.
94.14	0	800	1057	1	Chert	Late Stage Preform	Indeterminate Small Point	Possibly finished. Either a reworked point base or a point that was not thinned properly.
94.14	0	806	867	1	Meta-basalt	Early Stage Preform	Indeterminate Large Point	Minimal retouch.
2000.03	0	812	909	1	Basalt	Completed	U-shaped Base Triangular	
2000.03	0	813	909	1	Basalt	Completed	Straight Base Triangular	Possibly not finished.
94.14	0	817	1057	1	Obsidian	Completed	Concave Blade	Point is burned.
94.14	0	817	867	1	Rhyolite	Completed	San Pedro	Appears to have been attempted to be reworked into a small point.
2000.03	0	821	909	1	Basalt	Indeterminate	Indeterminate Small Point	
94.14	0	821	1192	1	Chert	Early Stage Preform	Indeterminate Small Point	
2000.03	0	822	909	2	Basalt	Completed	U-shaped Base Triangular	
2000.03	0	822	909	1	Basalt	Early Stage Preform	Indeterminate Small Point	
94.02	1	822	1112	1	Chert	Late Stage Preform	Indeterminate Small Point	
2000.03	0	828	909	1	Obsidian	Completed	Straight Base Triangular	Possibly a preform.
2000.03	0	829	909	1	Basalt	Completed	U-shaped Base Triangular	

Continued

Appendix A: GRIC-CRMP Projectile Point Assemblage (Continued)

Project	Task	Specimen	Site	Subspecimen	Material	Stage	Point Style	Comments
2000.03	0	831	909	1	Basalt	Early Stage Preform	Indeterminate Large Point	Appears to be a reworked flake that was patinated.
94.14	0	831	931	1	Basalt	Late Stage Preform	Indeterminate Small Point	
94.02	1	832	1112	1	Chert	Completed	Indeterminate Small Point	
94.14	0	832	931	1	Basalt	Completed	Long Triangular	
94.14	0	833	931	1	Chalcedony	Completed	Concave Base Triangular	
94.14	0	834	931	1	Chert	Completed	U-shaped Base Triangular	Possibly Straight Base Triangular.
94.14	0	835	1057	1	Obsidian	Completed	Concave Blade	Tip appears broken and reworked.
94.14	0	835	931	1	Chert	Completed	Indeterminate Large Point	
94.14	0	836	931	1	Obsidian	Completed	Straight Base Triangular	Government Mountain obsidian.
2000.03	0	837	909	1	Chert	Completed	Straight Base Triangular	Quite possibly a preform broken during manufacture.
94.14	0	837	931	1	Obsidian	Completed	Intermediate Side-Notched	
94.14	0	838	931	1	Chalcedony	Completed	U-shaped Base Triangular	
2000.03	0	840	909	1	Basalt	Completed	U-shaped Base Triangular	Maybe unfinished--possibly Straight Base Triangular.
2000.03	0	841	909	1	Basalt	Completed	U-shaped Base Triangular	Possibly ground!
2000.03	0	845	909	1	Obsidian	Early Stage Preform	Indeterminate Small Point	
94.14	0	845	870	1	Basalt	Early Stage Preform	Indeterminate Large Point	Has minimal retouch.
94.14	0	845	931	1	Chalcedony	Completed	Concave Blade	
94.14	0	846	931	1	Chalcedony	Late Stage Preform	Indeterminate Small Point	
94.14	0	847	931	1	Obsidian	Completed	U-shaped Base Triangular	
94.14	0	848	870	1	Chert	Early Stage Preform	Indeterminate Large Point	

Continued

Appendix A: GRIC--CRMP Projectile Point Assemblage *(Continued)*

Project	Task	Specimen	Site	Subspecimen	Material	Stage	Point Style	Comments
94.14	0	853	871	1	Basalt	Late Stage Preform	Indeterminate Small Point	
94.14	0	858	931	1	Chert	Early Stage Preform	Indeterminate Small Point	Minimally retouched, step fractures and steep edge angles prevented further thinning.
94.14	0	859	931	1	Basalt	Indeterminate	Intermediate Side-Notched	Does not fit the typology well.
94.14	0	872	871	1	Basalt	Completed	Stemmed Teardrop	One shoulder is abrupt and one is sloping. This point is possible a late prehistoric spear point.
94.14	0	873	871	1	Chert	Completed	Chiricahua	Tip and one ear have been reworked. Fairly well made for a Chiricahua.
94.14	0	873	931	1	Basalt	Early Stage Preform	Indeterminate Small Point	Possibly a drill midsection.
94.14	0	875	931	1	Obsidian	Late Stage Preform	Indeterminate Small Point	Possibly finished but is only partly thinned.
94.14	0	876	442	2	Obsidian	Completed	Straight Base Triangular	Possibly glass, possibly unfinished--rather thick.
94.14	0	876	442	3	Obsidian	Completed	Straight Blade Serrated	
94.14	0	876	931	1	Basalt	Completed	Straight Base Triangular	
94.14	0	877	931	1	Chert	Completed	U-shaped Base Triangular	
94.14	0	878	931	1	Chert	Completed	U-shaped Base Triangular	Base only moderately concave, could be classified as Straight Base Triangular.
94.14	0	879	931	1	Basalt	Completed	Straight Base Triangular	Could be classified as U-shaped Base Triangular. Possibly unfinished--crude and poorly thinned.
94.14	0	880	191	1	Basalt	Completed	San Jose-Pinto A	Does not fit typology well. Has a straight-sided short stem with a concave base and serrated edges.
94.14	0	881	191	1	Rhyolite	Completed	Chiricahua	Appears to be the base of a large side-notched point. Differs greatly from "standard" Chiricahua.
2000.03	0	886	909	1	Basalt	Completed	U-shaped Base Triangular	
2000.03	0	888	909	1	Basalt	Completed	Cienega Long	Stem is longer and narrower than most Cienega points; possibly unfinished or just poorly made.
94.14	0	889	931	1	Chalcedony	Completed	U-shaped Base Triangular	Possibly unfinished, crude and poorly thinned.
2000.03	0	890	909	1	Obsidian	Completed	U-shaped Base Triangular	Large for U-shaped Base Triangular point.

Continued

Appendix A: GRIC-CRMP Projectile Point Assemblage (*Continued*)

Project	Task	Specimen	Site	Subspecimen	Material	Stage	Point Style	Comments
94.14	0	892	931	1	Chert	Completed	Straight Base Triangular	Tip has impact fracture. Well thinned.
94.14	0	893	931	1	Obsidian	Completed	U-shaped Base Triangular	Could be classified as serrated--edge is irregular.
94.14	0	894	931	1	Obsidian	Completed	Intermediate Side-Notched	Almost mid-side notched.
94.14	0	896	931	1	Obsidian	Completed	U-shaped Base Triangular	
94.14	0	911	874	1	Rhyolite	Completed	San Pedro	Poor example of a San Pedro--stem is narrower than it should be.
94.14	0	920	1120	1	Obsidian	Early Stage Preform	Indeterminate Small Point	
2000.03	0	922	909	1	Chert	Completed	San Jose-Pinto A	
94.14	0	923	877	1	Chalcedony	Completed	Indeterminate Small Point	Could be a large point--stem is narrow but thick. Tip appears to have been reworked into a drill. Probably a side-notched point of some type.
94.14	0	925	1120	1	Chert	Completed	Concave Blade	
2000.03	0	928	909	1	Basalt	Late Stage Preform	Straight Base Triangular	Possibly finished but crude.
2000.03	0	929	909	1	Chert	Completed	Straight Base Triangular	Possibly unfinished, very crude.
2000.03	0	930	909	1	Chert	Completed	U-shaped Base Triangular	
2000.03	0	931	909	1	Basalt	Completed	Straight Base Triangular	Very crude, possibly unfinished.
2000.03	0	935	909	1	Chert	Completed	U-shaped Base Triangular	
2000.03	0	936	909	1	Obsidian	Completed	U-shaped Base Triangular	Possibly unfinished, very crude.
94.14	0	943	1120	1	Chalcedony	Completed	Flanged	Could be classified as side-notched.
94.14	0	945	1120	2	Quartz	Completed	Straight Blade Serrated	Possibly Concave Blade.
2000.03	0	964	909	1	Obsidian	Completed	U-shaped Base Triangular	
2000.03	0	972	909	1	Chert	Completed	U-shaped Base Triangular	
2000.03	0	977	909	1	Obsidian	Completed	Bulbous Base	Possibly unfinished, very crude.
2000.03	0	978	909	1	Obsidian	Completed	U-shaped Base Triangular	

Continued

Appendix A: GRIC--CRMP Projectile Point Assemblage *(Continued)*

Project	Task	Specimen	Site	Subspecimen	Material	Stage	Point Style	Comments
2000.03	0	986	909	2	Obsidian	Completed	U-shaped Base Triangular	
2000.03	0	986	909	3	Obsidian	Completed	U-shaped Base Triangular	
2000.03	0	986	909	4	Chert	Completed	Indeterminate Large Point	Thickness and width suggest this is the tip of a large point.
2000.03	0	993	909	1	Rhyolite	Completed	Indeterminate Large Point	This artifact is possibly the stem of a large point, but both edges appear to be snap fractures. One of the two snapped edges appears to possibly have been reworked.
2000.03	0	994	909	1	Chert	Late Stage Preform	Indeterminate Small Point	Possibly finished but appears to have a single notch suggesting it broke during notching.
2000.03	0	995	909	1	Obsidian	Completed	U-shaped Base Triangular	
2000.03	0	996	909	1	Chert	Early Stage Preform	Indeterminate Small Point	Very crude.
94.14	0	999	744	1	Chalcedony	Early Stage Preform	Indeterminate Large Point	Possibly a small point preform.
94.14	0	1002	744	1	Chert	Early Stage Preform	Indeterminate Small Point	
2000.03	0	1004	909	1	Basalt	Completed	Thin Triangular	Possibly unfinished.
94.14	0	1004	1153	1	Rhyolite	Completed	San Pedro	Evidence for reworking is limited. Point has edge beveling and is short for how thick it is. The material is possibly chert but appears to have phenocrysts.
94.14	0	1006	196	1	Basalt	Early Stage Preform	Indeterminate Large Point	Very crude--possibly a knife.
94.14	0	1012	332	3	Chert	Early Stage Preform	Indeterminate Small Point	
94.14	0	1018	744	1	Chert	Late Stage Preform	Straight Base Triangular	Possibly finished, but base is not retouched and is irregular.
2000.03	0	1035	909	1	Chert	Completed	Indeterminate Small Point	Possibly a Cienega Stemmed--too fragmentary to tell.
94.14	0	1036	332	1	Rhyolite	Early Stage Preform	Indeterminate Large Point	
2000.03	0	1071	909	1	Chert	Completed	Straight Base Triangular	
2000.03	0	1072	909	1	Chalcedony	Early Stage Preform	Indeterminate	
2000.03	0	1073	909	1	Quartz	Completed	Indeterminate	Strange and crude point--does not fit the typology--is an idiosyncratic style, possibly a Ceramic period spear point.

Continued

Appendix A: GRIC-CRMP Projectile Point Assemblage (*Continued*)

Project	Task	Specimen	Site	Subspecimen	Material	Stage	Point Style	Comments
2000.03	0	1076	909	1	Basalt	Completed	U-shaped Base Triangular	
2000.03	0	1077	909	1	Rhyolite	Completed	Straight Base Triangular	Very crude--minimally retouched--possibly unfinished but has a regular shape.
2000.03	0	1078	909	1	Chert	Late Stage Preform	Indeterminate	Possibly has light usewear and could be a unifacial tool.
2000.03	0	1080	909	1	Chert	Late Stage Preform	Indeterminate Small Point	Very crude and has a twist that would greatly complicate hafting, suggesting this point is unfinished.
94.14	0	1080	528	2	Chert	Completed	Middle Side-Notched	Minimally thinned.
2000.03	0	1081	909	1	Obsidian	Completed	U-shaped Base Triangular	Looks like it could be transitional between the Straight Base Triangular and U-shaped base styles--base is probably concave as a result of attempting to thin the lower portion of the point for hafting.
94.14	0	1083	194	1	Meta-basalt	Completed	Indeterminate Large Point	Thick CaCo₃ encrustation.
2000.03	0	1086	194	1	Obsidian	Early Stage Preform	Indeterminate Small Point	Very crude.
2000.03	0	1090	1238	1	Obsidian	Completed	U-shaped Base Triangular	One ear missing.
2000.03	0	1092	1238	1	Obsidian	Late Stage Preform	Indeterminate Small Point	Possibly finished but very crude.
94.14	0	1093	744	1	Chert	Late Stage Preform	Indeterminate Small Point	
2000.03	0	1094	1238	1	Basalt	Completed	Flanged	Possibly unfinished--a little crude. Not the best example of Flanged.
2000.03	0	1095	1238	1	Basalt	Late Stage Preform	Indeterminate Small Point	
2000.03	0	1096	1238	1	Obsidian	Early Stage Preform	Indeterminate Small Point	Minimal retouch.
94.14	0	1104	192	1	Rhyolite	Completed	San Pedro	Well-made large point.
94.14	0	1110	194	1	Obsidian	Completed	Flanged	Almost side-notched. Possibly Concave Blade.
94.14	0	1129	269	1	Chert	Late Stage Preform	Indeterminate Small Point	Step fractures resulted in an isolated mass.
94.14	0	1133	744	1	Basalt	Late Stage Preform	Straight Base Triangular	
94.14	0	1161	1120	1	Chert	Completed	Stemmed Barbed	Tip missing.
94.14	0	1169	1120	1	Chert	Late Stage Preform	Indeterminate Small Point	Appears to have snapped during thinning--possibly a large point.

Continued

Appendix A: GRIC-CRMP Projectile Point Assemblage *(Continued)*

Project	Task	Specimen	Site	Subspecimen	Material	Stage	Point Style	Comments
94.14	0	1170	1120	1	Obsidian	Completed	Indeterminate Small Point	Almost side-notched. Possibly Concave Blade Serrated.
94.14	0	1174	1120	1	Basalt	Early Stage Preform	Indeterminate Small Point	Extremely crude. Has wide shallow side notches but base is irregular and appears unfinished.
94.14	0	1182	1120	1	Chert	Completed	Eccentric	Has been heat altered, probably after it was made. Possibly a drill, as blade is very narrow; but it lacks opposed steep angle retouch, suggesting it is not a drill. Very unusual style with 2 barbs.
2000.03	0	1183	1239	1	Basalt	Completed	San Jose-Pinto B	Not the best example of a San Jose.
94.14	0	1183	1120	1	Chert	Completed	Indeterminate Small Point	Either corner-notched or stemmed.
2000.03	0	1187	1239	1	Quartz	Late Stage Preform	Indeterminate Large Point	Very crude.
94.14	0	1197	1120	1	Quartzite	Completed	Flanged	Is very large for an arrow point, but does not appear to be an Archaic style. Possibly unfinished.
94.14	0	1203	1120	1	Basalt	Completed	Straight Blade Serrated	Possibly unfinished, quite thick and large. Could be U-shaped Base Triangular.
94.14	0	1208	1120	1	Chert	Completed	Indeterminate Small Point	Possibly Narrow Side-Notched based on size.
94.14	0	1214	1120	1	Quartz	Early Stage Preform	Indeterminate Small Point	
94.14	0	1226	1120	1	Obsidian	Completed	U-shaped Base Triangular	Very heavily ground on one face with minor grinding on the other.
94.14	0	1228	1120	1	Quartz	Completed	Indeterminate Small Point	Hard to classify this fragment. Point may have had unusual notching.
94.14	0	1251	485	1	Chalcedony	Completed	U-shaped Base Triangular	
2000.03	0	1254	909	1	Basalt	Completed	Straight Base Triangular	Possibly ground.
2000.03	0	1255	909	1	Chert	Completed	U-shaped Base Triangular	Crude and very small point.
2000.03	0	1259	909	1	Obsidian	Completed	Straight Base Triangular	
94.14	0	1260	485	1	Chert	Early Stage Preform	Indeterminate Small Point	Point appears to be water-worn? Possibly could be usewear but is too uniform.
94.14	0	1264	750	1	Chert	Completed	U-shaped Base Triangular	Looks like an U-shaped Base Triangular point but is too thick and wide.

Continued

Appendix A: GRIC-CRMP Projectile Point Assemblage (Continued)

Project	Task	Specimen	Site	Subspecimen	Material	Stage	Point Style	Comments
94.14	0	1267	485	1	Basalt	Completed	Concave Base Triangular	
94.14	0	1270	1120	1	Chert	Completed	Flanged	Possibly not reworked but appears to be the base of a side-notched point that was modified into an unnotched point.
94.14	0	1273	485	1	Chalcedony	Completed	Concave Base Triangular	Possibly unfinished, as it is rather thick but blade edges are regular.
94.14	0	1282	485	1	Chert	Completed Late Stage	Long Triangular	Could be classified as Concave Base Triangular.
94.14	0	1283	485	1	Chert	Preform	Indeterminate	
94.14	0	1289	485	1	Chalcedony	Late Stage Preform	Indeterminate Small Point	
94.14	0	1303	544	1	Rhyolite	Completed	Indeterminate Large Point	Appears reworked (possibly into a Gypsum-style contracting base) but is too fragmentary to be certain.
94.14	0	1304	545	1	Chert	Completed	San Pedro	Edge beveling suggests reworking.
94.14	0	1305	545	1	Chert	Completed	Gypsum	Better made than most Gypsum points. Possibly very fine-grained quartzite.
94.14	0	1307	1120	1	Chalcedony	Completed	Straight Base Triangular	
94.14	0	1307	1120	2	Chalcedony	Early Stage Preform	Indeterminate Small Point	
94.14	0	1316	485	1	Chert	Completed	Wide Side-Notched	
94.14	0	1324	485	1	Chert	Completed	Cienega Short	
94.14	0	1329	1120	1	Chert	Completed	Wide Side-Notched	Tip and one ear missing.
94.14	0	1344	1123	1	Chert	Completed	Intermediate Side-Notched	One ear missing.
94.14	0	1361	554	1	Rhyolite	Completed	San Pedro	Small for a San Pedro. Very crude point, reworked.
94.14	0	1374	295	2	Chert	Completed	Thin Triangular	Possibly unfinished. Very minimal retouch.
94.14	0	1374	295	3	Chert	Completed	Thin Triangular	Does not fit typology well.
94.14	0	1374	295	4	Chert	Early Stage Preform	Indeterminate Small Point	Very crude. Maker attempted to thin the point from the base.
94.14	0	1375	500	1	Basalt	Completed	Stemmed Teardrop	Possibly unfinished. Very crude.
94.14	0	1380	295	2	Chert	Early Stage Preform	Indeterminate	Very minimally retouched.
94.14	0	1380	295	3	Chert	Late Stage Preform	Indeterminate Small Point	
94.14	0	1398	1125	1	Siltstone	Completed	Chiricahua	Tip has impact fracture.

Continued

Appendix A: GRIC-CRMP Projectile Point Assemblage *(Continued)*

Project	Task	Specimen	Site	Subspecimen	Material	Stage	Point Style	Comments
94.14	0	1414	1126	1	Chert	Completed	Middle Side-Notched	Has a bit of a curve--possibly unfinished.
94.14	0	1424	485	1	Chert	Completed	Intermediate Side-Notched	
94.14	0	1437	485	1	Chert	Early Stage Preform	Indeterminate Large Point	
94.14	0	1455	485	1	Chert	Completed	Concave Blade	
94.14	0	1461	485	1	Chert	Early Stage Preform	Indeterminate Small Point	
94.14	0	1501	445	2	Chert	Late Stage Preform	Indeterminate Small Point	
94.14	0	1515	310	1	Obsidian	Completed	U-shaped Base Triangular	Possibly Straight Base Triangular, base is only moderately concave and point is large. Could also be unfinished, as it is only partially retouched.
94.14	0	1515	310	2	Obsidian	Completed	U-shaped Base Triangular	Possibly Straight Base Triangular.
94.14	0	1515	310	3	Obsidian	Completed	Indeterminate Large Point	Appears to be a reworked large projectile point. Base and tip have been reworked.
94.14	0	1528	743	1	Obsidian	Completed	Flanged	Is a low-side-notch point that broke through the notches and was reworked into a narrower unnotched point.
94.14	0	1547	311	1	Chalcedony	Completed	U-shaped Base Triangular	
94.14	0	1572	755	1	Chert	Completed	Cienega Short	Possibly not usewear, clearly reworked.
94.14	0	1579	757	1	Rhyolite	Completed	Stemmed Teardrop	Similar to untyped stemmed large points.
94.14	0	1590	759	1	Rhyolite	Completed	Silver Lake	
94.14	0	1597	513	1	Basalt	Completed	Cienega Stemmed	Good example of Cienega Stemmed.
94.14	0	1598	513	1	Basalt	Completed	Shouldered Teardrop	Strange point, teardrop shaped with a straight stem.
94.14	0	1599	513	1	Basalt	Completed	Cienega Long	Very well made. Slightly serrated.
94.14	0	1613	194	1	Basalt	Completed	Stemmed Teardrop	Possibly unfinished. Could have dark varnish, but Indeterminate.
94.14	0	1618	743	1	Obsidian	Completed	Straight Blade Serrated	Possibly Concave Blade Serrated. Could be partly finished--is a little thick.
94.14	0	1620	743	1	Obsidian	Completed	Intermediate Side-Notched	Government Mountain obsidian.
94.14	0	1621	515	1	Meta-basalt	Early Stage Preform	Indeterminate Large Point	Crude biface--probably a large point preform.

Continued

Appendix A: GRIC-CRMP Projectile Point Assemblage *(Continued)*

Project	Task	Specimen	Site	Subspecimen	Material	Stage	Point Style	Comments
94.14	0	1624	743	1	Chert	Late Stage Preform	Indeterminate Large Point	Clearly unfinished. Too irregular to classify as Cortaro.
94.14	0	1628	760	1	Chert	Completed	Chiricahua	Is more similar to small points but too large. Has fossil inclusions. Very well made; much better thinned than most Chiricahua points.
94.14	0	1643	743	1	Meta-basalt	Late Stage Preform	Indeterminate Large Point	Possibly finished but blade margins irregular.
94.14	0	1645	516	1	Basalt	Completed	San Jose-Pinto A	Possibly unfinished--has large step fractures down the midline. Could be classified as side- or corner notched.
94.14	0	1646	194	1	Chert	Completed	Cienega Short	Appears heat treated. Possibly rhyolite.
94.14	0	1654	516	1	Obsidian	Completed	Flanged	Very crude and possibly unfinished.
94.14	0	1655	516	1	Basalt	Completed	Chiricahua	Possibly serrated. Crude point and possibly unfinished.
94.14	0	1669	751	1	Basalt	Completed	San Jose-Pinto A	Very crude and possibly unfinished. May not be San Jose.
94.14	0	1670	751	1	Basalt	Completed	Cienega Long	Could be Cienega Short.
94.14	0	1671	1135	1	Quartz	Completed	Indeterminate Small Point	Large point size but small point style. Does not fit the typology.
94.14	0	1697	568	1	Rhyolite	Completed	Chiricahua	Possibly not finished but is notched--has many step fractures.
94.14	0	1710	760	1	Basalt	Completed	Indeterminate Small Point	
94.14	0	1724	570	1	Chert	Completed	Eccentric	Tip appears to have been used as a perforator.
94.14	0	1725	570	1	Chert	Completed	Narrow Side-Notched	
94.14	0	1727	570	1	Basalt	Completed	Indeterminate Large Point	
94.14	0	1728	570	1	Chert	Completed	Concave Blade	
94.14	0	1729	570	1	Chert	Completed	U-shaped Base Triangular	Tip and one ear missing. Base is not as concave as other U-shaped Base Triangular points.
94.14	0	1733	743	1	Obsidian	Completed	Indeterminate Small Point	Side-notched.
94.14	0	1743	1137	1	Chert	Completed	Flanged	Unusual point probably a reworked Archaic style. Appears to have been a side or corner notched point that broke and was reworked.
94.14	0	1744	743	1	Obsidian	Completed	Wide Side-Notched	One face appears burned.
94.14	0	1745	743	1	Chert	Completed	Concave Blade	Possibly should be Eccentric style.
94.14	0	1746	743	1	Chert	Late Stage Preform	Indeterminate Small Point	
94.14	0	1756	578	1	Chert	Completed	Narrow Side-Notched	

Continued

Appendix A: GRIC-CRMP Projectile Point Assemblage (Continued)

Project	Task	Specimen	Site	Subspecimen	Material	Stage	Point Style	Comments
94.14	0	1787	1139	1	Chert	Completed	Indeterminate Large Point	Quite possibly a preform.
94.14	0	1792	1139	1	Chert	Completed	Gypsum	Base and one shoulder broken--possibly not a Gypsum.
94.14	0	1821	1139	1	Chert	Completed	Indeterminate Small Point	Material is actually silicified wood. Possibly U-shaped Base Triangular.
94.14	0	1829	1139	1	Chert	Completed	U-shaped Base Triangular	
94.14	0	1830	1139	1	Obsidian	Completed	Thin Triangular	Quite possibly unfinished. Very thin but minimally retouched. Could have been worked further.
94.14	0	1841	1139	1	Obsidian	Completed	Intermediate Side-Notched	Possibly glass.
94.14	0	1845	744	1	Glass	Completed	U-shaped Base Triangular	Possibly obsidian. Very crude and possibly unfinished.
94.14	0	1845	744	2	Chert	Completed	U-shaped Base Triangular	Possibly rhyolite.
94.14	0	1862	1139	1	Rhyolite	Late Stage Preform	San Pedro	Point is possibly finished and simply very poorly made. Quite possibly is not an Archaic point. Does not fit the typology well. Bad example of San Pedro.
94.14	0	1863	592	1	Chert	Completed	Cienega Short	Similar to a Cienega stemmed but is corner-notched.
94.14	0	1867	1139	2	Obsidian	Late Stage Preform	Indeterminate Small Point	Possibly finished and very crude (would be a Straight Base Triangular probably), but one edge is only partially retouched.
94.14	0	1867	1139	1	Obsidian	Late Stage Preform	Indeterminate Small Point	Possibly finished and just very crude.
94.14	0	1875	595	1	Obsidian	Late Stage Preform	Indeterminate	Possibly a large point. Very crude and irregular, suggesting it is unfinished, but it has notches. Possibly a reworked tip. Point has wear suggesting it is old (Archaic?).
94.14	0	1884	1139	1	Chert	Completed	U-shaped Base Triangular	Fairly crude. Not a very good example of U-shaped Base Triangular--base isn't deeply concave.
94.14	0	1887	485	1	Obsidian	Completed	Middle Side-Notched	Possibly Upper Side-Notched.
94.14	0	1888	485	1	Chert	Completed	U-shaped Base Triangular	
94.14	0	1896	1139	1	Rhyolite	Early Stage Preform	Indeterminate	Extremely heavy wear. May have never been used as a projectile point.
94.14	0	1897	1139	1	Chert	Completed	Thin Triangular	Could be a preform, as it is large, but it could have readily been thinned and/or shaped further.
94.14	0	1898	1139	1	Obsidian	Early Stage Preform	Indeterminate Small Point	

Continued

Appendix A: GRIC-CRMP Projectile Point Assemblage (*Continued*)

Project	Task	Specimen	Site	Subspecimen	Material	Stage	Point Style	Comments
94.14	0	1900	1139	1	Chert	Early Stage Preform	Indeterminate Small Point	
94.14	0	1904	775	1	Chert	Early Stage Preform	Indeterminate Small Point	Very early stage preform with major step fractures.
94.14	0	1915	1139	1	Chert	Completed	Cienega Short	Broken through the notches. Tentatively a Cienega Short.
94.14	0	1918	1139	1	Chert	Late Stage Preform	Indeterminate Small Point	Looks like they attempted to make low side-notches but failed on one side due to thickness.
94.14	0	1919	1139	1	Basalt	Completed	San Jose-Pinto B	Does not fit the typology well. Possibly a Jay or San Pedro. Unusual material that is possibly rhyolite.
94.14	0	1926	1139	1	Obsidian	Completed	Intermediate Side-Notched	Unusual point. Very deeply concave base and could be classified as mid- side-notched.
94.14	0	1926	275	1	Basalt	Completed	Indeterminate Large Point	Possibly a small bifacial knife.
94.14	0	1928	0	1	Basalt	Completed	Straight Base Triangular	Possibly unfinished.
94.14	0	1929	1139	1	Chert	Late Stage Preform	Indeterminate	Probably a small point preform.
94.14	0	1944	1139	1	Obsidian	Early Stage Preform	Indeterminate Small Point	
94.14	0	1946	1139	1	Obsidian	Completed	U-shaped Base Triangular	Could be Straight Base Triangular--base is only moderately concave and point lacks serration.
94.14	0	1948	1139	1	Obsidian	Completed	Intermediate Side-Notched	Well made.
94.14	0	1950	1139	1	Chert	Completed	U-shaped Base Triangular	Good example of style, but both ears are missing.
94.14	0	1950	775	1	Obsidian	Late Stage Preform	U-shaped Base Triangular	Point may have broken when ears were being made. Possibly finished but the margins are irregular.
94.14	0	1951	1139	1	Chert	Late Stage Preform	Cortaro	Has trimmed base--probably a preform for a corner-notched point. Edge angles are too steep along one margin and has a number of step and hinge fractures.
94.14	0	1952	1139	1	Obsidian	Late Stage Preform	Indeterminate Small Point	The preform probably snapped during manufacture--is only partially retouched.
94.14	0	1953	1139	1	Glass	Completed	U-shaped Base Triangular	Quite possibly unfinished. Very crude like most glass points.
94.14	0	1954	775	1	Obsidian	Completed	Intermediate Side-Notched	
94.14	0	1955	1139	1	Chert	Completed	Indeterminate	Is very large for a arrow point but is an arrow style. Could be unfinished as base has minimal retouch.

Continued

Appendix A: GRIC-CRMP Projectile Point Assemblage (Continued)

Project	Task	Specimen	Site	Subspecimen	Material	Stage	Point Style	Comments
94.14	0	1956	1139	1	Chert	Completed	U-shaped Base Triangular	
94.14	0	1957	1139	1	Chert	Completed	U-shaped Base Triangular	
94.14	0	1957	485	1	Chalcedony	Completed	Stemmed Tanged	Very crude. Possibly unfinished. Small for a older point but does not fit more recent styles.
94.14	0	1958	1139	1	Basalt	Completed	U-shaped Base Triangular	
94.14	0	1958	775	1	Chert	Late Stage Preform	Gypsum	Possibly finished very crude point. May not be a Gypsum.
94.14	0	1959	1139	1	Obsidian	Completed	Straight Base Triangular	Possibly unfinished, a little thick.
94.14	0	1960	1139	1	Glass	Completed	Straight Base Triangular	Very crude, possibly unfinished. Brown glass.
94.14	0	1960	1139	2	Glass	Completed	Straight Base Triangular	Very crude, possibly unfinished.
94.14	0	1961	1139	1	Chert	Late Stage Preform	U-shaped Base Triangular	Possibly finished and very crude, but edge is irregular. Has a step fracture and isolated mass.
94.14	0	1962	775	1	Obsidian	Early Stage Preform	Indeterminate Small Point	
94.14	0	1963	1139	1	Obsidian	Completed	U-shaped Base Triangular	
94.14	0	1964	1139	1	Chert	Completed	U-shaped Base Triangular	Good example of style.
94.14	0	1964	775	1	Chert	Late Stage Preform	Straight Base Triangular	Point is serrated, suggesting it is finished, but it is too thick for an arrow point and too small (and the wrong style) for an Archaic point.
94.14	0	1965	1139	1	Rhyolite	Completed	Cienega Short	Style is difficult to determine. Point appears to have been reworked, was possibly a San Pedro, but probably originally a Cienega Long.
94.14	0	1967	485	1	Chert	Late Stage Preform	Indeterminate Small Point	
94.14	0	1968	485	1	Chert	Completed	Straight Base Triangular	Possibly unfinished.
94.14	0	1972	1139	1	Chert	Completed	U-shaped Base Triangular	
94.14	0	1973	1139	1	Obsidian	Completed	U-shaped Base Triangular	Tip has impact fracture.

Continued

Appendix A: GRIC-CRMP Projectile Point Assemblage (Continued)

Project	Task	Specimen	Site	Subspecimen	Material	Stage	Point Style	Comments
94.14	0	1978	775	1	Chert	Completed	U-shaped Base Triangular	
94.14	0	1980	775	1	Chert	Early Stage Preform	Indeterminate Small Point	Possibly finished because it has serrations at the tip, but has very minimal retouch and step fractures along one edge precluding further thinning.
94.14	0	1982	1139	2	Obsidian	Early Stage Preform	Indeterminate Small Point	
94.14	0	1982	1139	9	Obsidian	Early Stage Preform	Indeterminate Small Point	
94.14	0	1982	1139	6	Chert	Late Stage Preform	Indeterminate Large Point	Possibly finished. Base is trimmed, suggesting the point could be a preform for a corner-notched point.
94.14	0	1982	1139	3	Chert	Late Stage Preform	Indeterminate	Possibly finished.
94.14	0	1982	1139	5	Chert	Late Stage Preform	Indeterminate Small Point	Possibly for a large point.
94.14	0	1982	1139	7	Chert	Late Stage Preform	Indeterminate Large Point	
94.14	0	1985	1139	1	Obsidian	Early Stage Preform	Indeterminate Small Point	Possibly a large point preform but is a little too small.
94.14	0	1989	775	1	Chert	Early Stage Preform	Indeterminate Large Point	Possibly a small point preform. Has 3 major step fractures that precluded further thinning.
94.14	0	1992	1139	1	Chert	Completed	U-shaped Base Triangular	Is very thick and possibly unfinished.
94.14	0	1993	1139	1	Basalt	Completed	U-shaped Base Triangular	Possibly ground--Indeterminate as it is under the label.
94.14	0	1994	1139	1	Chert	Completed	U-shaped Base Triangular	
94.14	0	1995	1139	1	Obsidian	Completed	Bulbous Base	Crude and possibly unfinished.
94.14	0	1996	1139	1	Obsidian	Completed	Intermediate Side-Notched	Doesn't fit the typology well. Poorly notched and crude, could be unfinished.
94.14	0	2001	1139	1	Chalcedony	Late Stage Preform	U-shaped Base Triangular	Very crude. Similar to U-shaped Base Triangular style but is way too large. Possibly finished and a late spear point that is very poorly made.
94.14	0	2002	1139	1	Chert	Late Stage Preform	U-shaped Base Triangular	Possibly finished.
94.14	0	2004	1139	1	Obsidian	Completed	U-shaped Base Triangular	Possibly unfinished--rather thick and somewhat irregular edges.
94.14	0	2005	1139	2	Obsidian	Early Stage Preform	Indeterminate Small Point	Early stage preform broken during manufacture.

Continued

Appendix A: GRIC-CRMP Projectile Point Assemblage (Continued)

Project	Task	Specimen	Site	Subspecimen	Material	Stage	Point Style	Comments
94.14	0	2005	1139	3	Chert	Early Stage Preform	Indeterminate Small Point	Minimally retouched on one face. Lower portion of preform appears to have snapped off during manufacture.
94.14	0	2009	1139	1	Obsidian	Completed	U-shaped Base Triangular	Good example of style.
94.14	0	2009	720	2	Basalt	Completed	Silver Lake	Small for this style--possibly Gypsum.
94.14	0	2009	720	1	Chert	Late Stage Preform	Indeterminate Large Point	Base is trimmed in a similar fashion to other large point preforms--this must be part of the production sequence. Has step fractures that precluded further thinning.
94.14	0	2012	1139	1	Chert	Late Stage Preform	Indeterminate Large Point	Has a large hinge fracture and step fractures as well.
94.14	0	2013	1139	1	Chert	Completed	Straight Base Triangular	Possibly unfinished.
94.14	0	2016	621	1	Basalt	Completed	San Jose-Pinto A	Could be reworked.
94.14	0	2018	1139	1	Basalt	Completed	Shouldered Teardrop	A little small for a large point but doesn't look like a small point style.
94.14	0	2019	1139	1	Basalt	Completed	Chiricahua	Appears to be a reworked point tip.
94.14	0	2019	304	1	Basalt	Completed	Gypsum	Does not fit typology well. Possibly not an Archaic point.
94.14	0	2020	1139	1	Obsidian	Completed	U-shaped Base Triangular	Good example of style.
94.14	0	2021	1139	1	Basalt	Completed	San Pedro	Has edge beveling. The serration appears to have been added when it was reworked. The point has edge beveling.
94.14	0	2022	1139	1	Obsidian	Completed	Intermediate Side-Notched	
94.14	0	2023	1139	1	Chert	Completed	Eccentric	Possibly Concave Blade
94.14	0	2024	1139	1	Chert	Early Stage Preform	Indeterminate Small Point	Is only partially thinned--discarded due to step fractures.
94.14	0	2026	1139	2	Chert	Late Stage Preform	Indeterminate Small Point	Broke during notching.
94.14	0	2026	1139	3	Obsidian	Early Stage Preform	Indeterminate Small Point	Minimally retouched Bifacial Thinning Flake. Possibly not a point preform.
94.14	0	2026	1139	4	Obsidian	Late Stage Preform	Intermediate Side-Notched	Broken during notching.
94.14	0	2026	1139	5	Chert	Late Stage Preform	Indeterminate Small Point	Probably broken during manufacture.
94.14	0	2026	1139	6	Basalt	Completed	Cienega Stemmed	Similar to Cienega Stemmed but the stem contracts slightly. Possibly a Gypsum point.

Continued

Appendix A: GRIC-CRMP Projectile Point Assemblage (Continued)

Project	Task	Specimen	Site	Subspecimen	Material	Stage	Point Style	Comments
94.14	0	2027	1139	1	Rhyolite	Completed	Shouldered Teardrop	Strange point. Does not fit the typology. Possibly a late prehistoric spear point.
94.14	0	2029	1139	1	Obsidian	Completed	Indeterminate Small Point	
94.14	0	2029	782	1	Basalt	Completed	Straight Base Triangular	Possibly U-shaped Base Triangular, but base is only slightly concave.
94.14	0	2031	1139	1	Chert	Completed	U-shaped Base Triangular	Large for U-shaped Base Triangular, but otherwise a good example of the style.
94.14	0	2032	1139	1	Chert	Early Stage Preform	Indeterminate Small Point	Very poorly thinned.
94.14	0	2032	775	1	Chert	Early Stage Preform	Straight Base Triangular	
94.14	0	2033	1139	1	Obsidian	Completed	Indeterminate Small Point	Broken through the notches. Government Mountain obsidian.
94.14	0	2033	1139	2	Obsidian	Completed	Indeterminate Small Point	Either middle or low side-notching.
94.14	0	2033	1139	3	Obsidian	Completed	Flanged	Tip is impact fractured.
94.14	0	2033	1139	4	Obsidian	Completed	Indeterminate Small Point	Possibly unfinished, one face has minimal retouch.
94.14	0	2035	1139	1	Obsidian	Completed	Indeterminate Small Point	Doesn't fit the typology. Similar to Desert side-notched or Plains tri-notch.
94.14	0	2036	1139	1	Rhyolite	Completed	Cienega Long	Does not fit the typology well. Barbs are too short for Cienega Long. Notching is more similar to San Pedro.
94.14	0	2042	775	1	Obsidian	Late Stage Preform	Straight Base Triangular	Possibly finished, but the margins are irregular.
94.14	0	2048	1139	2	Obsidian	Late Stage Preform	U-shaped Base Triangular	Edges are irregular, suggesting the point isn't finished. May have broken during final shaping of the point, but could be finished and just crude.
94.14	0	2048	1139	3	Chert	Indeterminate	Indeterminate Large Point	Possibly a preform but has usewear. May not be Archaic--could be a utilized biface.
94.14	0	2048	1139	4	Obsidian	Completed	Indeterminate Small Point	Has a basal notch. Similar to other side-notched points from 1139 with deeply concave bases--they don't fit the typology--similar to Desert Side-Notch or Plains Tri-Notch
94.14	0	2048	1139	6	Obsidian	Completed	Straight Base Triangular	Possibly unfinished--rather crude, has cortex on one corner. Very difficult to orientate the point, as it is almost an equilateral triangle.
94.14	0	2048	1139	7	Obsidian	Late Stage Preform	Indeterminate Small Point	Probably broken during notching.

Continued

Appendix A: GRIC-CRMP Projectile Point Assemblage *(Continued)*

Project	Task	Specimen	Site	Subspecimen	Material	Stage	Point Style	Comments
94.14	0	2048	1139	1	Chalcedony	Late Stage Preform	Indeterminate Small Point	
94.14	0	2048	1139	8	Obsidian	Late Stage Preform	Indeterminate Small Point	Government Mountain obsidian. Base may have snapped during notching.
94.14	0	2052	806	1	Chert	Completed	Concave Base Triangular	Possibly U-shaped Base Triangular.
94.14	0	2065	1139	1	Obsidian	Completed	Intermediate Side-Notched	Small fragment. Possibly different style.
94.14	0	2070	196	1	Basalt	Completed	San Pedro	The polish is largely on one face. The evidence for reworking is equivocal.
94.14	0	2071	1139	1	Rhyolite	Late Stage Preform	Indeterminate Large Point	Is possibly a finished point but has irregular margins and several step fractures that resulted in a large isolated mass. Tip appears to have been used as a drill.
94.14	0	2072	1139	1	Tuff	Late Stage Preform	Indeterminate Large Point	Possibly finished but has irregular margins and is curved.
94.14	0	2073	1139	1	Obsidian	Completed	Straight Base Triangular	Looks like U-shaped Base Triangular style except the base is not concave.
94.14	0	2074	1139	1	Chert	Completed	Cortaro	Very possibly unfinished. Has a number of step fractures and a fairly thick isolated mass near the base. Is otherwise regular in outline, and the base is trimmed (not enough to be a stem) in a similar fashion to other large unnotched points.
94.14	0	2077	1139	2	Basalt	Early Stage Preform	Indeterminate Large Point	Possibly a perforator.
94.14	0	2080	1139	1	Basalt	Completed	U-shaped Base Triangular	One face may be ground.
94.14	0	2081	1139	1	Chert	Early Stage Preform	Indeterminate Small Point	
94.14	0	2082	1139	1	Chert	Completed	U-shaped Base Triangular	One ear missing.
94.14	0	2084	807	1	Basalt	Completed	U-shaped Base Triangular	Possibly Straight Base Triangular.
94.14	0	2087	1139	1	Chert	Completed	Chiricahua	Tip has definitely been used.
94.14	0	2096	779	1	Chert	Completed	Middle Side-Notched	Very unusual double-notched point. Doesn't fit typology well.
94.14	0	2098	1139	1	Obsidian	Completed	U-shaped Base Triangular	Possibly unfinished--edge is a little irregular.
94.14	0	2101	194	1	Chert	Completed	Narrow Side-Notched	

Continued

Appendix A: GRIC-CRMP Projectile Point Assemblage (*Continued*)

Project	Task	Specimen	Site	Subspecimen	Material	Stage	Point Style	Comments
94.14	0	2102	194	1	Chert	Completed	Indeterminate Small Point	Probably side-notched.
94.14	0	2123	196	1	Obsidian	Completed	Wide Side-Notched	Well-made point.
94.14	0	2147	807	1	Chert	Completed	Straight Base Triangular	Possibly unfinished. Rather thick.
94.14	0	2148	807	1	Obsidian	Completed	Concave Blade	Wider than most Concave Blade.
2000.16	0	2194	787	1	Obsidian	Completed	Indeterminate Small Point	Possibly unfinished. Rather thick.
2000.16	0	2196	787	1	Quartzite	Completed	Indeterminate Large Point	Appears to be a large point based on the thickness.
2000.16	0	2199	787	1	Chert	Early Stage Preform	Indeterminate Small Point	Possibly a drill base but doesn't have opposed step angle retouch.
2000.16	0	2240	787	1	Chert	Completed	Intermediate Side-Notched	Tip and one ear missing. Rather crude and possibly unfinished.
2000.16	0	2248	787	1	Obsidian	Completed	Intermediate Side-Notched	Doesn't fit the typology well.
94.14	0	2279	441	1	Chert	Completed	San Pedro	Very tip missing. Appears heat treated.
94.14	0	2318	740	1	Rhyolite	Completed	Cienega Long	Somewhat crude point.
2000.16	0	2321	787	1	Chert	Completed	Wide Side-Notched	
2000.16	0	2333	787	2	Obsidian	Completed	Indeterminate Small Point	
94.14	0	2357	740	1	Chert	Completed	U-shaped Base Triangular	
94.14	0	2358	740	1	Meta-basalt	Completed	Stemmed Teardrop	A little small for an archaic point--possibly more recent.
94.14	0	2378	450	1	Basalt	Late Stage Preform	Indeterminate Large Point	Has a trimmed edges at the base--the base itself is not thinned, suggesting this was a preform for a corner-notched(?) point that broke during manufacture.
94.14	0	2531	786	1	Basalt	Completed	U-shaped Base Triangular	
94.14	0	2544	786	1	Chert	Late Stage Preform	Long Triangular	
94.14	0	2545	786	2	Obsidian	Completed	Indeterminate Small Point	Government Mountain obsidian
94.14	0	2545	786	3	Obsidian	Completed	Indeterminate Small Point	Possibly glass.

Continued

Appendix A: GRIC-CRMP Projectile Point Assemblage *(Continued)*

Project	Task	Specimen	Site	Subspecimen	Material	Stage	Point Style	Comments
2000.16	0	2555	787	1	Obsidian	Completed	U-shaped Base Triangular	Possibly Straight Base Triangular.
94.14	0	2589	738	1	Chert	Completed	Middle Side-Notched	Might be a Historic period point.
94.14	0	2607	646	1	Chert	Completed	Indeterminate	Possibly a Cienega-style arrow point. Base is broken so it is unclear if this was a stemmed or corner-notched point.
94.14	0	2679	522	1	Chert	Completed	Indeterminate Small Point	Chert looks heat-treated.
94.14	0	2720	740	1	Chert	Early Stage Preform	Indeterminate Small Point	Tip is broken, and this preform may have been discarded as a result.
94.14	0	2731	740	1	Chert	Early Stage Preform	Indeterminate	Early stage preform that could have been intended for a large or small point.
94.14	0	2751	656	1	Chert	Completed	Stemmed Tanged	Possibly corner notched--stem is missing. Point style may be incorrect.
94.14	0	2863	1157	1	Chert	Completed	Intermediate Side-Notched	
94.14	0	2876	1157	1	Chert	Completed	Stemmed Shouldered	Point has been burned--possibly heat-treated or went through a cremation fire.
94.14	0	2877	1157	1	Chert	Completed	Intermediate Small Point	
94.14	0	2878	1157	1	Chert	Completed	Indeterminate Small Point	
94.14	0	2879	1157	1	Chert	Completed	Narrow Side-Notched	Good example of the style. Tip missing.
94.14	0	2886	1157	1	Obsidian	Completed	Intermediate Side-Notched	One ear missing.
94.14	0	2910	1157	1	Rhyolite	Completed	Silver Lake	
94.14	0	2918	1157	1	Chert	Completed	Concave Blade	
94.14	0	2919	1157	1	Chalcedony	Completed	Concave Blade	
94.14	0	2920	1157	1	Chalcedony	Late Stage Preform	Indeterminate Small Point	Possibly a reworked point tip but is irregular. Good example of an attempt to thin a point from the base--this failed due to step fracturing.
94.14	0	2935	1157	1	Chert	Completed	Stemmed Barbed	Strange little point--almost corner-notched.
94.14	0	2985	1157	1	Chert	Completed	Eccentric	Unique point. Possibly Concave Blade.
94.14	0	3019	1157	1	Chert	Completed	Intermediate Side-Notched	Point appears to have heated after manufacture--has pot-lid fractures and the surface coloration appears to have been altered due to extreme heating.
94.14	0	3034	1157	1	Obsidian	Completed	Indeterminate Small Point	
94.14	0	3035	1157	1	Chert	Completed	Concave Blade	

Continued

Appendix A: GRIC-CRMP Projectile Point Assemblage (*Continued*)

Project	Task	Specimen	Site	Subspecimen	Material	Stage	Point Style	Comments
94.14	0	3046	1157	1	Obsidian	Completed	Concave Blade	
94.14	0	3047	1157	1	Chalcedony	Completed	U-shaped Base Triangular	
94.14	0	3083	1157	1	Chert	Early Stage Preform	Indeterminate Small Point	An early stage preform.
94.14	0	3086	1157	1	Chert	Completed	Wide Side-Notched	
94.14	0	3103	1157	1	Rhyolite	Completed	Chiricahua	Tip appears reworked but not into a different point style (reworking probably occurred during the Archaic).
94.14	0	3124	1157	1	Chalcedony	Completed	Concave Blade	
94.14	0	3145	1157	1	Chalcedony	Early Stage Preform	Indeterminate Small Point	
94.14	0	3148	1157	1	Basalt	Completed	San Jose-Pinto A	Varies somewhat from San Jose points in the Borderlands area. Has an expanding stem rather than a concave side stem. It does have the projections at the shoulders.
94.14	0	3185	1157	1	Chert	Completed	Stemmed Tanged	
94.14	0	3236	1157	1	Chert	Completed	Flanged	
94.14	0	3304	1157	2	Obsidian	Early Stage Preform	Indeterminate Small Point	
94.14	0	3309	1157	1	Rhyolite	Completed	Intermediate Side-Notched	
94.14	0	3344	1157	1	Rhyolite	Completed	Intermediate Side-Notched	Has a basal notch.
94.14	0	3346	1157	1	Obsidian	Completed	Indeterminate Small Point	
94.14	0	3347	1157	1	Obsidian	Early Stage Preform	Indeterminate Small Point	
94.14	0	3349	1157	1	Obsidian	Completed	Intermediate Side-Notched	
94.14	0	3407	1157	1	Obsidian	Completed	U-shaped Base Triangular	
94.14	0	3411	1157	1	Obsidian	Early Stage Preform	Indeterminate Small Point	Possibly finished but very crude.
94.14	0	3412	1157	1	Chert	Completed	U-shaped Base Triangular	Possibly Concave Blade.
94.14	0	3469	1157	1	Chalcedony	Completed	Intermediate Side-Notched	Appears to be a large point based on size but is a small point style.

Continued

Appendix A: GRIC-CRMP Projectile Point Assemblage (Continued)

Project	Task	Specimen	Site	Subspecimen	Material	Stage	Point Style	Comments
94.14	0	3477	1157	1	Chert	Late Stage Preform	Cortaro	Appears to be a preform. Has numerous step fractures on both faces along one margin. Could possibly even have been intended to be a small point, but the step fractures precluded further thinning so it was discarded.
94.14	0	3487	1157	1	Chert	Completed	Eccentric	
94.14	0	3508	1157	1	Basalt	Completed	Chiricahua	Possibly not an Archaic point--this is a small point style but is way too large. Possibly a late prehistoric spear point.
94.14	0	3533	1157	1	Chert	Late Stage Preform	Indeterminate Small Point	
94.14	0	3553	1157	1	Obsidian	Completed	Intermediate Side-Notched	
94.14	0	3610	1157	1	Basalt	Late Stage Preform	Indeterminate Small Point	
94.14	0	3684	1157	1	Chert	Completed	Long Triangular	
94.14	0	3719	1157	1	Chert	Late Stage Preform	Indeterminate Small Point	
94.14	0	3720	1157	1	Obsidian	Completed	Flanged	Possibly unfinished.
94.14	0	3721	1157	1	Chert	Completed	Bulbous Base	
94.14	0	3754	1157	1	Basalt	Completed	Indeterminate Small Point	Tip appears reworked. Possibly originally an Archaic point
94.14	0	3766	1157	1	Obsidian	Completed	Intermediate Side-Notched	Probably Government Mountain obsidian.
94.14	0	3767	1157	1	Obsidian	Completed	Intermediate Side-Notched	
94.14	0	3789	1157	1	Obsidian	Early Stage Preform	Indeterminate Small Point	
94.14	0	3841	1157	1	Obsidian	Completed	Intermediate Side-Notched	Has basal notch.
94.14	0	3847	1157	1	Chert	Late Stage Preform	Indeterminate Small Point	Very crude point but could be finished.
94.14	0	3850	1157	1	Obsidian	Completed	Intermediate Side-Notched	
94.14	0	3851	1157	1	Chert	Completed	Middle Side-Notched	
94.14	0	3852	1157	1	Obsidian	Late Stage Preform	Indeterminate Small Point	
94.14	0	3860	1157	1	Obsidian	Late Stage Preform	Indeterminate Small Point	Probably a reworked point fragment.

Continued

Appendix A: GRIC-CRMP Projectile Point Assemblage *(Continued)*

Project	Task	Specimen	Site	Subspecimen	Material	Stage	Point Style	Comments
94.14	0	3879	1157	1	Obsidian	Completed	Straight Base Triangular	Possibly unfinished point, is very crude.
94.14	0	3880	1157	1	Chert	Completed	San Jose-Pinto A	Possibly a small point.
94.14	0	3906	194	1	Chert	Completed	Indeterminate Large Point	Possibly snapped during manufacture and is only partly finished.
94.14	0	3913	1157	1	Obsidian	Completed	Concave Blade	
94.14	0	3945	1157	1	Obsidian	Late Stage Preform	Indeterminate Small Point	Too thick and edge angles prevented further thinning.
94.14	0	3951	1157	1	Basalt	Completed	Flanged	Well made for basalt.
94.14	0	4042	1157	1	Chert	Completed	Intermediate Side-Notched	Unusual point--wide base and narrow blade.
94.14	0	4053	1157	1	Obsidian	Completed	Intermediate Side-Notched	
94.14	0	4070	1157	1	Obsidian	Completed	Straight Base Triangular	
94.14	0	4097	1157	1	Chert	Completed	Flanged	
94.14	0	4102	1157	1	Obsidian	Completed	Straight Base Triangular	
94.14	0	4105	1157	2	Obsidian	Early Stage Preform	Indeterminate Small Point	Probably snapped during manufacture.
94.14	0	4140	1157	1	Obsidian	Completed	Intermediate Side-Notched	
94.14	0	4151	1157	1	Chert	Completed	Cienega Long	Has numerous step fractures. Shoulders are less barbed than usual for Cienega, but stem is extremely similar.
94.14	0	4156	1157	1	Obsidian	Completed	Indeterminate Small Point	
94.14	0	4253	1157	1	Obsidian	Completed	Indeterminate Small Point	
94.14	0	4259	1157	2	Obsidian	Late Stage Preform	Indeterminate Small Point	
94.14	0	4276	1157	1	Chert	Completed	Indeterminate Small Point	
94.14	0	4281	1157	1	Rhyolite	Completed	Intermediate Side-Notched	
94.14	0	4283	1157	1	Obsidian	Completed	Intermediate Side-Notched	

Continued

Appendix A: GRIC-CRMP Projectile Point Assemblage (Continued)

Project	Task	Specimen	Site	Subspecimen	Material	Stage	Point Style	Comments
94.14	0	4344	1157	1	Chert	Completed	Indeterminate Small Point	
94.14	0	4436	1157	1	Chert	Completed	Upper Side-Notched	Almost not notched--has wide and shallow notches.
94.14	0	4501	194	1	Rhyolite	Completed	Cienega Long	Well-made point. Base slightly broken.
94.14	0	4502	194	1	Chert	Completed	Concave Blade	Unusually deep serrations. Possibly should be classed as Eccentric.
94.14	0	4503	1167	1	Obsidian	Completed	Concave Blade	Possibly Straight Blade Serrated or U-shaped Base Triangular
94.14	0	4510	194	1	Rhyolite	Completed	Chiricahua	May not be Chiricahua-- has three notches. Could be unfinished.
94.14	0	4539	1164	1	Obsidian	Completed	Intermediate Side-Notched	Very crude; may not be finished, but has two notches. Strange material possibly not obsidian--may be heat-treated.
94.14	0	4614	1164	1	Obsidian	Completed	Intermediate Side-Notched	Government Mountain obsidian.
94.14	0	4626	194	1	Chert	Completed	Stemmed Shouldered	Very shallow serrations. Tip and one ear missing.
94.14	0	4633	1166	1	Chert	Completed	Concave Blade	Looks like a small point style but is too large--does not fit the typology well.
94.14	0	4656	194	1	Quartzite	Completed	Chiricahua	
94.14	0	4683	1167	1	Chert	Completed	Cienega Short	Could be a Cienega Long.
94.14	0	4703	1167	1	Chert	Completed	Concave Blade	Classification is speculative, as point is very fragmentary--has heat-induced spalling
94.14	0	4704	1167	1	Chert	Early Stage Preform	Indeterminate Large Point	Possibly a small point preform.
94.14	0	4731	1167	1	Chert	Completed	Middle Side-Notched	Point is definitely reworked (has beveled edges and a edge angle change) and then broken again. Unclear what style the point originally was. The point should possibly be classified as unnotched as the notches are poorly defined.
94.14	0	4740	1167	1	Chert	Completed	Indeterminate Small Point	
94.14	0	4758	1167	1	Basalt	Completed	San Jose-Pinto A	
94.14	0	4777	1167	1	Basalt	Completed	San Jose-Pinto A	Reworking is questionable, but the point is rather thick for the length.
94.14	0	4811	1167	1	Obsidian	Completed	Wide Side-Notched	
94.14	0	4831	1167	1	Obsidian	Completed	Concave Blade	Good example of the style.
94.14	0	4899	1167	1	Chert	Completed	Narrow Side-Notched	Might be a dart point. One ear missing.
94.14	0	4918	1167	1	Obsidian	Completed	Concave Blade	Rather small for this type.
94.14	0	4965	1167	1	Rhyolite	Completed	Cienega Long	Has beveled edges--appears to be a reworked Cienega Long.
94.14	0	5034	776	1	Chert	Completed	Middle Side-Notched	Broken through the notches. Deeply concave base.

Continued

Appendix A: GRIC-CRMP Projectile Point Assemblage (*Continued*)

Project	Task	Specimen	Site	Subspecimen	Material	Stage	Point Style	Comments
94.14	0	5046	776	1	Obsidian	Completed	Flanged	Almost side-notched. Does not fit the typology well.
94.14	0	5053	776	1	Basalt	Completed	San Jose-Pinto A	Possibly a small point--stem is narrow.
94.14	0	5109	194	1	Chert	Completed	Indeterminate Small Point	Appears to be a reworked base, might originally have been corner notched and much larger. Tip has impact factor.
94.14	0	5125	1174	1	Basalt	Completed	San Pedro	Possibly a Cienega Long.
94.14	0	5162	1175	1	Obsidian	Completed	U-shaped Base Triangular	
94.14	0	5165	1175	2	Obsidian	Completed	Intermediate Side-Notched	The artifact is a reworked tip of a side-notched point, which broke through the notches.
94.14	0	5192	1175	1	Chalcedony	Completed	Indeterminate Small Point	
94.14	0	5214	1175	1	Obsidian	Completed	Straight Blade Serrated	
94.14	0	5230	1175	1	Chert	Completed	Thin Triangular	
94.14	0	5259	1175	2	Obsidian	Completed	Intermediate Side-Notched	Government Mountain obsidian.
94.14	0	5259	1175	3	Obsidian	Completed	Intermediate Side-Notched	
94.14	0	5288	1175	2	Obsidian	Completed	Straight Blade Serrated	
94.14	0	5353	1204	1	Obsidian	Late Stage Preform	U-shaped Base Triangular	Very crude, possibly finished.
94.14	0	5509	1207	1	Quartzite	Completed	San Pedro	Part of one edge may be serrated. Point has heavy $CaCo_3$ encrustation--has increased weight of point.
94.14	0	5510	1207	1	Basalt	Early Stage Preform	Indeterminate Small Point	Base is possibly broken but appears unfinished.
94.14	0	5536	1206	1	Chert	Completed	Narrow Side-Notched	Style is speculative due to the fragmentary nature of the point.
94.14	0	5594	1206	1	Chert	Completed	Wide Side-Notched	Could be a dart point.
94.14	0	5606	1212	1	Basalt	Completed	Chiricahua	The point is fragmentary and can only tentatively be assigned as Chiricahua. The tip and base (below what appear to be shallow side-notches) are missing.
94.14	0	5678	1214	1	Obsidian	Completed	Cienega Stemmed	Arrow point-size Cienega stemmed point.
94.14	0	5680	1213	2	Chert	Late Stage Preform	Indeterminate Small Point	

Continued

Appendix A: GRIC-CRMP Projectile Point Assemblage *(Continued)*

Project	Task	Specimen	Site	Subspecimen	Material	Stage	Point Style	Comments
94.14	0	5714	1157	1	Chalcedony	Completed	Intermediate Side-Notched	
94.14	0	5724	1157	1	Quartz	Completed	Indeterminate Small Point	
94.14	0	5731	1157	1	Obsidian	Late Stage Preform	Indeterminate Small Point	Not obvious why this wasn't completed, but this is clearly a preform.
94.14	0	5732	1157	1	Chert	Late Stage Preform	Indeterminate Small Point	Fragment that could be the base--appears to be a preform that snapped during manufacture.
94.14	0	5764	1157	1	Obsidian	Completed	Concave Blade	
94.14	0	5775	1157	1	Obsidian	Completed	Indeterminate Small Point	
94.14	0	5775	1157	2	Chert	Completed	U-shaped Base Triangular	
94.14	0	5775	1157	4	Chert	Late Stage Preform	Indeterminate Small Point	Minimally retouched bifacial thinning flake. Possibly a very crude completed point.
94.14	0	5804	1157	1	Chert	Completed	Intermediate Side-Notched	Possibly U-shaped Base Triangular.
94.14	0	5834	1157	2	Quartz	Completed	Wide Side-Notched	
94.14	0	5834	1157	3	Quartzite	Completed	San Jose-Pinto B	Very unusual material type; is green and white.
94.14	0	5862	1157	2	Obsidian	Late Stage Preform	Indeterminate Small Point	
94.14	0	5879	1157	2	Obsidian	Late Stage Preform	Indeterminate Small Point	Possibly a crude finished point.
94.14	0	5907	1157	2	Chalcedony	Completed	Intermediate Side-Notched	
94.14	0	5907	1157	3	Obsidian	Completed	U-shaped Base Triangular	Unusual point, one ear missing.
94.14	0	5931	1157	2	Rhyolite	Completed	San Pedro	Material is possibly chert but appears to have phenocrysts. Smaller than most San Pedro (more recent?), but the notching and base are correct for this style.
94.14	0	5942	1157	1	Chert	Late Stage Preform	Indeterminate Small Point	Possibly finished--tip may have broken during manufacture, which resulted in discard.
94.14	0	5976	1157	1	Chert	Completed	Thin Triangular	Possibly U-shaped Based Triangular
94.14	0	5977	1157	1	Basalt	Completed	Indeterminate Large Point	Possibly a small point but very thick.

Continued

Appendix A: GRIC-CRMP Projectile Point Assemblage (Continued)

Project	Task	Specimen	Site	Subspecimen	Material	Stage	Point Style	Comments
94.14	0	5978	1157	1	Chert	Late Stage Preform	Indeterminate Large Point	Has secondary thinning along a broken edge--given the small size this was probably done in an attempt to turn it into an arrow point. This is possibly a fragment from a finished point--difficult to tell what portion of the point this is.
94.14	0	5979	1157	1	Chert	Completed	U-shaped Base Triangular	
94.14	0	5983	1157	1	Chert	Completed	Long Triangular	Is long and narrow suggesting a drill but lacks opposed steep retouch and any usewear--was examined under microscope.
94.14	0	6014	1157	1	Obsidian	Completed	Middle Side-Notched	Very shallow notches.
94.14	0	6047	1157	2	Quartzite	Indeterminate	Indeterminate Large Point	Possibly not a projectile point tip; bifacial flaking not apparent and usewear is present.
94.14	0	6047	1157	3	Chert	Completed	U-shaped Base Triangular	Tip and one ear missing.
94.14	0	6068	1157	1	Obsidian	Completed	Intermediate Side-Notched	
94.14	0	6069	194	1	Obsidian	Completed	Straight Blade Serrated	Almost mid-side-notched.
94.14	0	6090	1157	2	Obsidian	Completed	Indeterminate Small Point	Strange little point. One ear missing. Does not fit the typology well.
94.14	0	6100	1157	1	Obsidian	Completed	Intermediate Side-Notched	Crude point. Possibly reworked older point.
94.14	0	6126	1157	2	Obsidian	Completed	U-shaped Base Triangular	
94.14	0	6126	1157	3	Chert	Completed	Narrow Side-Notched	
94.14	0	6126	1157	4	Chert	Completed	Intermediate Side-Notched	
94.14	0	6132	1157	1	Chert	Completed	San Jose-Pinto A	Possibly a small point.
94.14	0	6136	1157	1	Obsidian	Completed	Straight Blade Serrated	Possibly Concave Blade.
94.14	0	6150	1157	1	Chert	Completed	U-shaped Base Triangular	
94.14	0	6152	1157	1	Chert	Late Stage Preform	Indeterminate Large Point	Fragment--difficult to determine the point section.
94.14	0	6168	1217	1	Chert	Completed	Narrow Side-Notched	Appears to be a small point style but the stem is rather wide--also too thin for a large point.
94.14	0	6209	1157	1	Quartz	Completed	Concave Blade	

Continued

Appendix A: GRIC-CRMP Projectile Point Assemblage (*Continued*)

Project	Task	Specimen	Site	Subspecimen	Material	Stage	Point Style	Comments
94.14	0	6224	1157	1	Chert	Completed	Intermediate Side-Notched	
94.14	0	6225	1157	2	Quartz	Completed	Concave Blade	Thickness, serrations, and blade edge treatment all suggest this is the tip of a Concave Blade style point.
94.14	0	6226	1157	1	Obsidian	Completed	Straight Blade Serrated	
94.14	0	6282	1222	1	Obsidian	Late Stage Preform	Indeterminate Small Point	Possibly finished and side-notched.
94.14	0	6314	1157	1	Chert	Completed	Thin Triangular	
94.14	0	6326	1157	1	Chert	Completed	Intermediate Side-Notched	
94.14	0	6327	1157	1	Chert	Late Stage Preform	Indeterminate Large Point	Has isolated mass on both faces from step fractures.
94.14	0	6357	1157	1	Meta-basalt		Indeterminate Large Point	Has minimal retouch. Material is greenstone.
94.14	0	6358	1157	1	Chert	Completed	U-shaped Base Triangular	
94.14	0	6361	1157	1	Obsidian	Completed	Concave Blade	
94.14	0	6375	1157	2	Chert	Completed	Long Triangular	
94.14	0	6375	1157	3	Chalcedony	Completed	Concave Base Triangular	Possibly U-shaped Base Triangular. Unusual point.
94.14	0	6375	1157	4	Obsidian	Completed	Middle Side-Notched	
94.14	0	6375	1157	5	Chert	Early Stage Preform	Indeterminate	Heat-treated; has pot-lid fracture.
94.14	0	6378	1157	2	Obsidian	Completed	U-shaped Base Triangular	
94.14	0	6382	1157	1	Chert	Completed	U-shaped Base Triangular	Good example of U-shaped Base Triangular. One ear missing.
94.14	0	6383	1157	1	Chert	Completed	Indeterminate Small Point	
94.14	0	6384	1157	1	Chert	Completed	Indeterminate Small Point	Chert is heat-treated.
94.14	0	6385	1157	1	Chert	Completed	Eccentric	Unique point. Smaller than most other Eccentrics.
94.14	0	6386	1157	1	Chert	Completed	Upper Side-Notched	Very shallow notches--almost unnotched. Could be U-shaped Base Triangular

Continued

Appendix A: GRIC-CRMP Projectile Point Assemblage (Continued)

Project	Task	Specimen	Site	Subspecimen	Material	Stage	Point Style	Comments
94.14	0	6387	1157	1	Obsidian	Completed	Intermediate Side-Notched	Government Mountain obsidian. One ear missing.
94.14	0	6388	1157	1	Chert	Completed	Thin Triangular	Base is possibly broken. Minimally retouched.
94.14	0	6389	1157	1	Obsidian	Completed	Intermediate Side-Notched	Well-made small point. Very symmetrical base.
94.14	0	6407	1157	1	Chert	Completed	Middle Side-Notched	
94.14	0	6408	1157	1	Chert	Completed	Indeterminate Small Point	
94.14	0	6409	1157	1	Chert	Completed	Intermediate Side-Notched	Very deeply concave base. Unusual point, possibly not Intermediate Side-Notched.
94.14	0	6410	1157	1	Obsidian	Completed	Indeterminate Small Point	
94.14	0	6423	1157	1	Chert	Completed	U-shaped Base Triangular	
94.14	0	6426	1157	1	Obsidian	Completed	Upper Side-Notched	Shallow, comparatively wide notches.
94.14	0	6437	1157	1	Basalt	Completed	Indeterminate Small Point	Does not fit the typology. Unique point.
94.14	0	6483	522	3	Obsidian	Late Stage Preform	Indeterminate Small Point	
94.14	0	6483	522	4	Obsidian	Completed	Flanged	Doesn't fit the typology well--has wide shallow notches, and base doesn't flare like other Flanged points. Could be Wide Side-Notched.
94.14	0	6483	522	5	Obsidian	Completed	Intermediate Side-Notched	
94.14	0	6483	522	6	Obsidian	Completed	Straight Base Triangular	Possibly unfinished. Point does not fit typology well--has flanged base but is otherwise similar to Straight Base Triangular.
94.14	0	6483	522	7	Obsidian	Completed	Straight Base Triangular	Possibly U-shaped Base Triangular. Unusual point.
94.14	0	6501	522	1	Obsidian	Completed	Intermediate Side-Notched	
94.14	0	6501	522	2	Chert	Completed	Concave Blade	Smaller than most Concave Blade.
94.14	0	6501	522	3	Chert	Completed	Concave Blade	
94.14	0	6510	522	3	Obsidian	Completed	Indeterminate Small Point	Government Mountain obsidian. Possibly unfinished.
94.14	0	6512	522	3	Obsidian	Late Stage Preform	Indeterminate Small Point	Has a possible side-notch (possibly broken during notching), and the base appears to be broken.

Continued

Appendix A: GRIC-CRMP Projectile Point Assemblage *(Continued)*

Project	Task	Specimen	Site	Subspecimen	Material	Stage	Point Style	Comments
94.14	0	6533	523	1	Basalt	Completed	Stemmed Teardrop	Minimally retouched. Does not look a great deal like any other points.
94.14	0	7074	1157	2	Quartzite	Completed	San Pedro	This point is extremely similar to spec. #7959.1 from GR-1157; they could have been made by the same individual.
94.14	0	7076	1157	1	Basalt	Completed	San Jose-Pinto A	Very strange point. Has two pairs of notches in the stem. May be unique. Base appears broken
94.14	0	7079	1157	1	Chert	Completed	U-shaped Base Triangular	
94.14	0	7080	1157	1	Chalcedony	Completed	Indeterminate Small Point	
94.14	0	7082	1157	1	Chert	Completed	Stemmed Tanged	Unusual point.
94.14	0	7126	1157	1	Chert	Completed	Intermediate Side-Notched	Very shallow notches.
94.14	0	7169	1157	2	Obsidian	Late Stage Preform	Indeterminate Small Point	Government Mountain obsidian.
94.14	0	7178	1157	1	Obsidian	Completed	Intermediate Side-Notched	
94.14	0	7179	1157	1	Chert	Completed	Intermediate Side-Notched	
94.14	0	7209	1157	2	Quartzite	Completed	Indeterminate Large Point	Very unusual material, possibly should be conglomerate. Has large grains in a fine matrix. Point is possibly unfinished.
94.14	0	7228	1210	1	Chert	Completed	Stemmed Tanged	
94.14	0	7525	1157	1	Obsidian	Completed	Indeterminate Small Point	
94.14	0	7527	1157	1	Obsidian	Completed	Intermediate Side-Notched	Very small point.
94.14	0	7527	1157	3	Obsidian	Early Stage Preform	Indeterminate Small Point	
94.14	0	7528	1157	1	Obsidian	Completed	Intermediate Side-Notched	Probably Government Mountain obsidian. Very shallow notches.
94.14	0	7532	1157	1	Chert	Completed	Indeterminate Small Point	Heat altered, possibly burned in a cremation fire or treated--has pot-lid fractures and the base was split by heat.
94.14	0	7532	1157	2	Obsidian	Completed	Indeterminate Small Point	
94.14	0	7536	1157	3	Obsidian	Indeterminate	Indeterminate Small Point	Could be a side-notched early stage preform?

Continued

126

Appendix A: GRIC-CRMP Projectile Point Assemblage (*Continued*)

Project	Task	Specimen	Site	Subspecimen	Material	Stage	Point Style	Comments
94.14	0	7540	1157	2	Obsidian	Completed	Concave Base Triangular	
94.14	0	7540	1157	3	Obsidian	Completed	Indeterminate Small Point	Appears reworked, very crude--has wide shallow notches.
94.14	0	7556	1157	1	Obsidian	Completed	Intermediate Side-Notched	
94.14	0	7557	1157	1	Obsidian	Completed	Intermediate Side-Notched	Has basal notch. Unusual obsidian of unknown type.
94.14	0	7578	1157	2	Obsidian	Early Stage Preform	Indeterminate Small Point	Very crude with minimal retouch.
94.14	0	7578	1157	3	Obsidian	Late Stage Preform	Indeterminate Small Point	
94.14	0	7596	1157	2	Obsidian	Completed	Straight Base Triangular	Possibly unfinished as the artifact is curved.
94.14	0	7601	1157	1	Obsidian	Completed	Wide Side-Notched	
94.14	0	7632	1157	1	Chert	Completed	Middle Side-Notched	
94.14	0	7706	1157	1	Rhyolite	Completed	Indeterminate Small Point	Possibly a large point.
94.14	0	7750	1157	1	Obsidian	Completed	Concave Blade	
94.14	0	7783	1157	1	Chert	Completed	Wide Side-Notched	Possibly a different style.
94.14	0	7810	1157	1	Obsidian	Completed	U-shaped Base Triangular	Has a ground face. Very crude and may not be finished.
94.14	0	7837	1157	1	Chert	Completed	Narrow Side-Notched	
94.14	0	7882	1157	1	Chert	Completed	Concave Base Triangular	
94.14	0	7889	1157	1	Chert	Completed	Stemmed Tanged	
94.14	0	7911	1157	1	Basalt	Completed	Straight Base Triangular	Very crude and possibly unfinished.
94.14	0	7912	1157	1	Chert	Completed	U-shaped Base Triangular	
94.14	0	7913	1157	1	Chalcedony	Completed	Indeterminate Small Point	

Continued

Appendix A: GRIC-CRMP Projectile Point Assemblage *(Continued)*

Project	Task	Specimen	Site	Subspecimen	Material	Stage	Point Style	Comments
94.14	0	7933	1157	1	Chert	Completed	Straight Base Triangular	
94.14	0	7934	1157	1	Chert	Completed	Concave Blade	Possibly unfinished, as the artifact is rather thick and curved.
94.14	0	7935	1157	1	Chert	Completed	Middle Side-Notched	Unusual point.
94.14	0	7952	1157	2	Chert	Early Stage Preform	Indeterminate Small Point	Silicified wood. Very early stage preform and has minimal retouch.
94.14	0	7959	1157	1	Rhyolite	Completed	San Pedro	Very well made; similar to spec. #7074.2, another point from GR-1157.

APPENDIX B:
SCATTERPLOT MATRICES

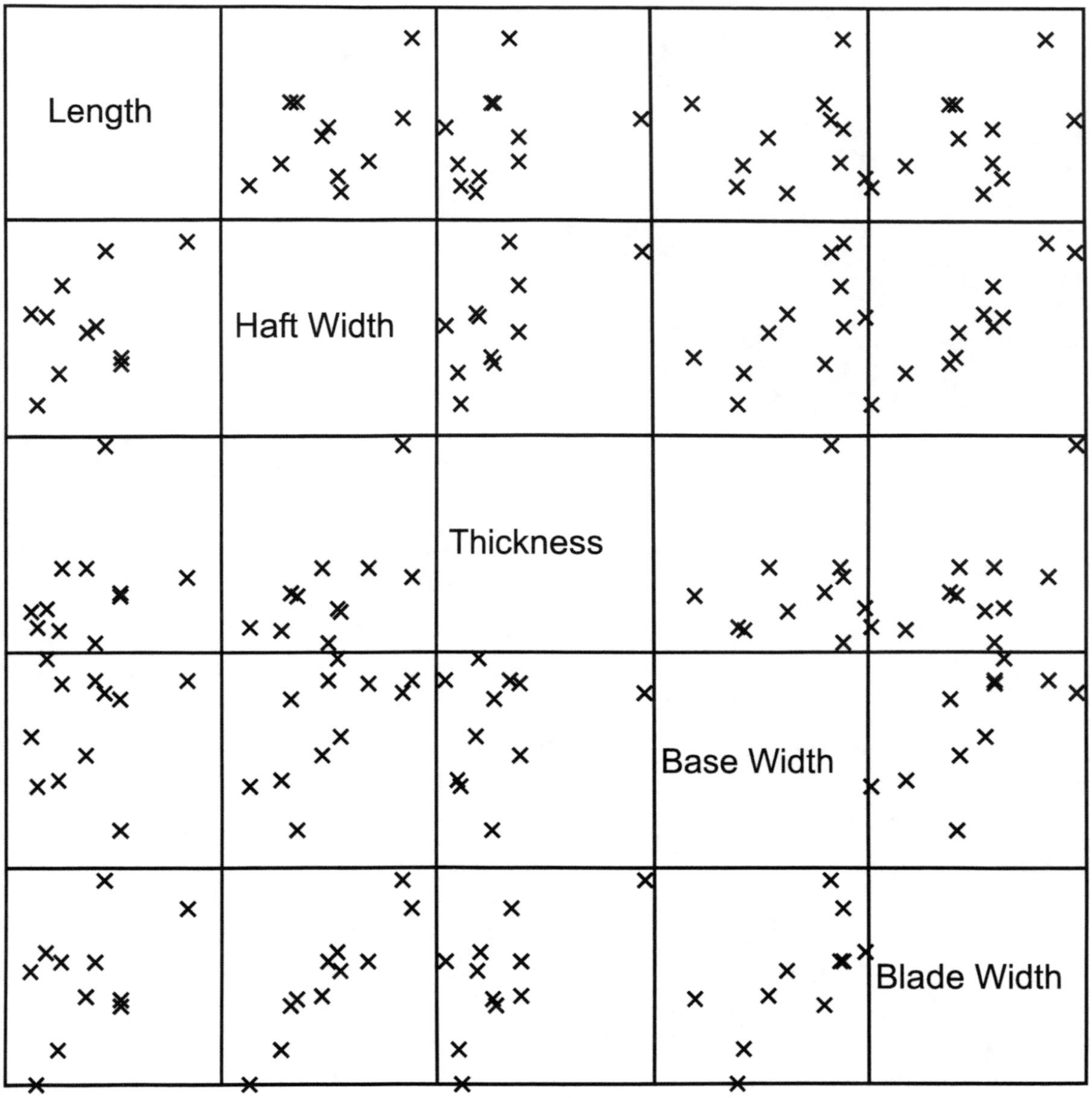

Figure B. 1. Chiricahua Scatterplot Matrix

Figure B. 2. San Jose--Pinto A Scatterplot Matrix

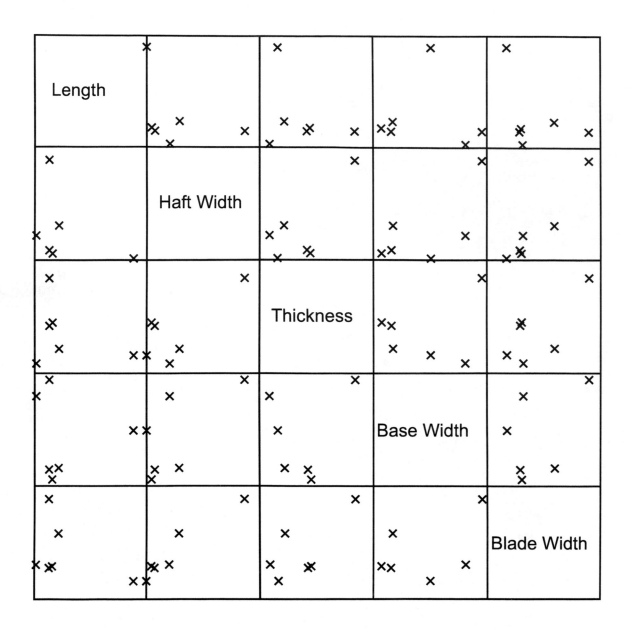

Figure B. 3. Pinto B Scatterplot Matrix

Figure B. 4. Gypsum Scatterplot Matrix

Figure B. 5. Cortaro Scatterplot Matrix

Figure B. 6. Shouldered Teardrop Scatterplot Matrix

Figure B. 7. Stemmed Teardrop Scatterplot Matrix

Figure B. 8. San Pedro Scatterplot Matrix

138

Figure B. 9. Cienega Long Scatterplot Matrix

Figure B. 10. Cienega Short Scatterplot Matrix

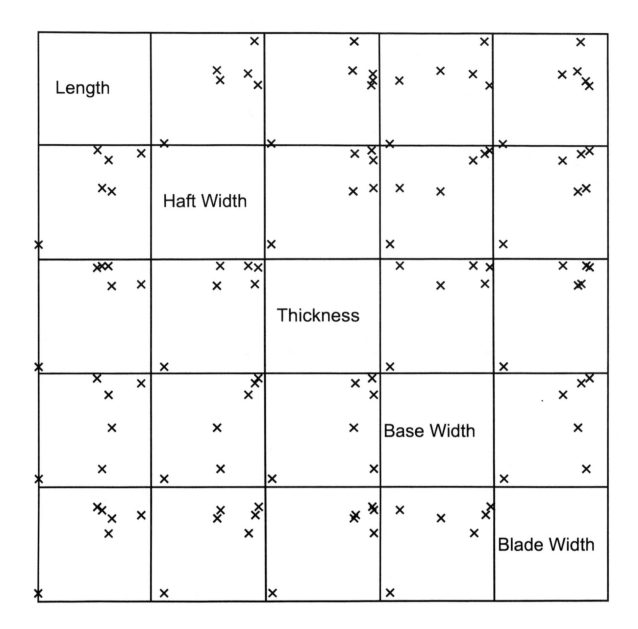

Figure B. 11. Cienega Stemmed Scatterplot Matrix

Figure B. 12. Wide Side-Notched Scatterplot Matrix

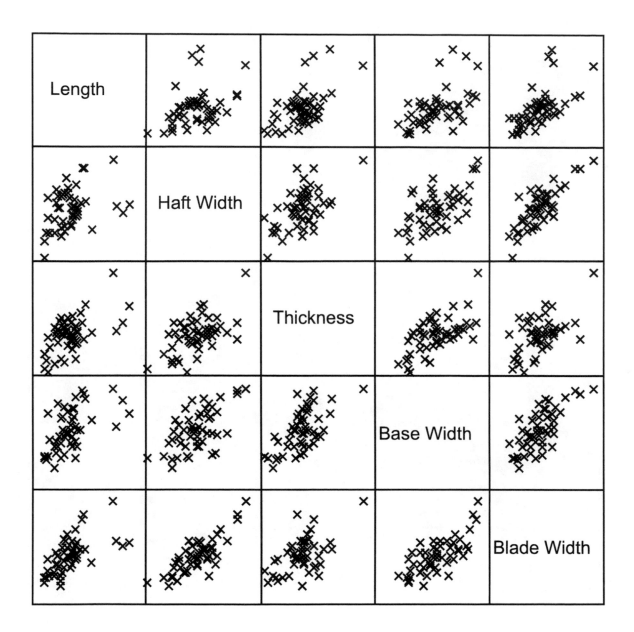

Figure B. 13. Intermediate Side-Notched Scatterplot Matrix

Figure B. 14. Middle Side-Notched Scatterplot Matrix

Figure B. 15. Flanged Scatterplot Matrix

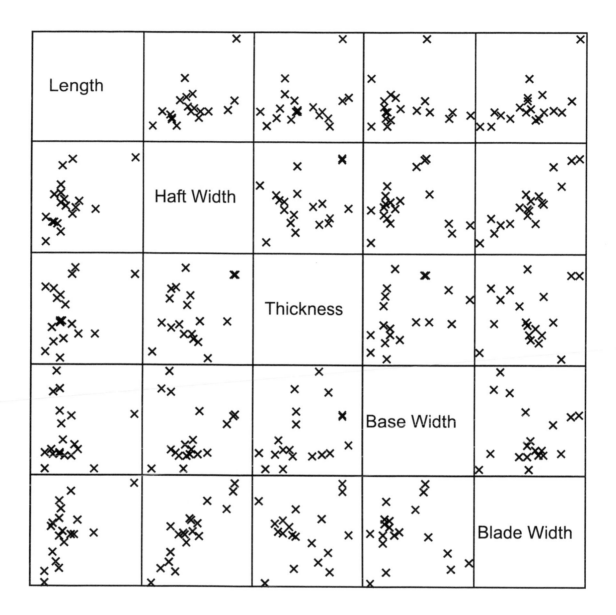

Figure B. 16. Concave Blade Scatterplot Matrix

Figure B. 17. Straight Blade Serrated Scatterplot Matrix

Figure B. 18. Concave Base Triangular Scatterplot Matrix

Figure B. 19. Thin Triangular Scatterplot Matrix

Figure B. 20 Long Triangular Scatterplot Matrix

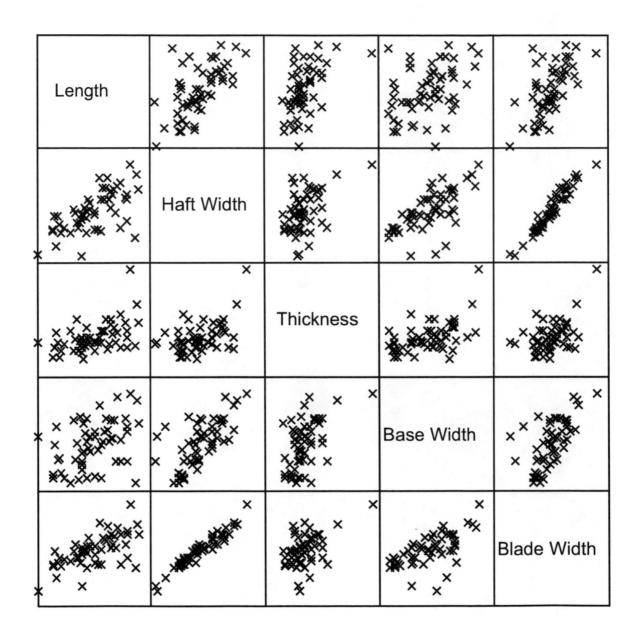

Figure B. 21. Straight Base Triangular Scatterplot Matrix

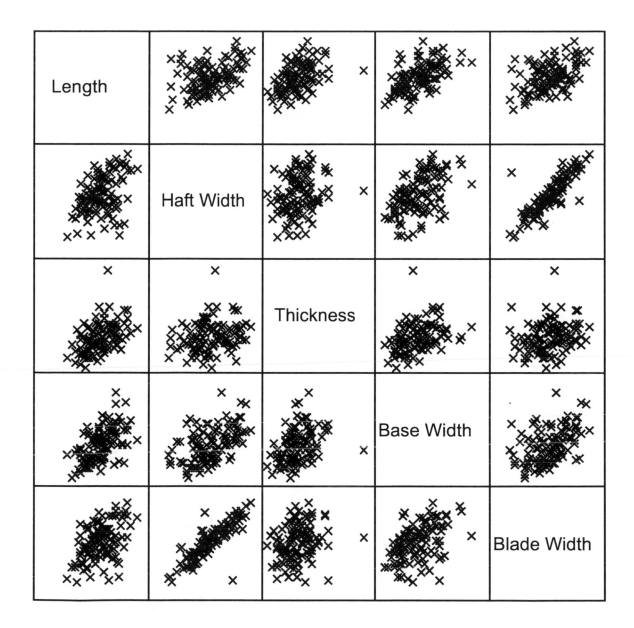

Figure B. 22. U-shaped Base Triangular Scatterplot Matrix